POWER OF GENTLENESS

FORDHAM UNIVERSITY PRESS   NEW YORK 2018

POWER OF GENTLENESS

Meditations on the Risk of Living

ANNE DUFOURMANTELLE

Translated by Katherine Payne and Vincent Sallé

This book was originally published in French as Anne Dufourmantelle, *Puissance de la douceur*, Copyright © Éditions Payot &
Rivages, 2013.

This work received the French Voices Award for excellence in
publication and translation. French Voices is a program created
and funded by the French Embassy in the United States and
FACE (French American Cultural Exchange). French Voices logo
designed by Serge Bloch.

Fordham University Press has no responsibility for the persistence or accuracy of URLs for external or third-party Internet
websites referred to in this publication and does not guarantee
that any content on such websites is, or will remain, accurate
or appropriate.

Fordham University Press also publishes its books in a variety
of electronic formats. Some content that appears in print may
not be available in electronic books.

Visit us online at www.fordhampress.com.

Library of Congress Control Number: 2017962402

Printed in the United States of America

20 19 18   5 4 3 2 1

First edition

for Maud

CONTENTS

FOREWORD:
PHILOSOPHY IN FURS

CATHERINE MALABOU

It is very rare for a book of philosophy to take the form of the subject matter of which it speaks: becoming substance when it addresses matter, geometry when it addresses surface, or even becoming impatient when it addresses time. *Power of Gentleness* achieves this incredible feat of being a gentle book. Of being a book "about" gentleness written "by" gentleness itself—a book where gentleness is simultaneously subject and object.

Gentleness had to be allowed to find its own voice, invent it, since, as Anne Dufourmantelle explains with great clarity, gentleness is never given. Which primarily means that it does not exist as philosophical concept. There is no technical definition of it. What is gentleness?

No thinker has ever considered the question thematically. Here gentleness must therefore present itself. But since rigid conceptual determination does not suit it, gentleness appears gradually through a series of tableaux that shape it. We are indeed amazed to discover a painterly writing. We witness in effect, marveling, in a writing that is painterly. Gardens, animals, a little girl playing with nativity figurines, "apricot-colored cardigan," "wings of butterflies coiled within their cocoon." . . . Ordinarily an artist draws before painting; this time it is the drawing that emerges from the painting. Throughout the journey, little by little, gentleness takes shape, it exists, it becomes thinkable at last.

To say that gentleness is not given also means that it is cultivated, that it is not "natural," even though nature can be gentle. That it is a virtue. And one might even say that once the reading journey is completed, gentleness appears as the very foundation of ethics, which is why "to attack gentleness is an unspeakable crime."

What then is gentleness about and what does it tell us? The title says it all! The tableaux-chapters reveal that in reality gentleness, though not a concept, though not a force, is nonetheless a powerful notion.

It has several names and several characteristics in all languages and all cultures. "In Latin *dulcis* signifies all possible gentlenesses, and *suavitas* describes God himself." In Greek, one finds the words *proates* and *praüs*, which the Vulgate translates as *mites*, poor and meek: "Blessed are the meek, for they shall inherit the earth," as one reads in the Beatitudes. "In Hebrew gentleness is expressed as: ''*navah*' and denotes one who is humble, low." We continue this journey with the Vedas through Gandhi's nonviolent resistance—one of the book's most beautiful tableaux, where one sees the Mahatma in dialogue with his three great interlocutors, Tolstoy, Ruskin, and Thoreau.

The light shared by all these tableaux and all these contexts is that of the sacred; I do not mean of the religious. Gentleness is "an attribute of God" before being a human value, but it can be learned, gained, and not venerated like a far-off divinity. Against this light, with a richness and an unexpected profusion—who would have been able to believe that gentleness was so fecund—of multiple political and moral motifs: justice, forgiveness, peace, generosity, listening.

But early on the question of the opposite of gentleness also arises. What is it? The answer is clear: violence, war, crime, massacre, genocide. . . . But one of the most surprising points of the book is the argument that the true enemy of gentleness is . . . gentleness. Fake gentleness, mawkishness, this passivity sold to us via every New Age commercial technique, of relaxation or of an overused meaning of "zen." This gentleness that one does not feel and that is another name for an indifference to authentic gentleness. "Gentleness sells. It is set before us in all its forms, everywhere, constantly. It is an economic argument paid to the account of whatever has nothing to do with it." Or later:

Gentleness is also divided in two by bodies of socio-economic control. On the carnal side, it is bastardized into silliness. On the spiritual side, into new age potion and other methods competing to make us believe that it is enough to believe in them in order for everything to work. Theories of self-improvement and pursuit of happiness participate in spite of themselves in this grand marketplace of "well-being" that refuses to enter into negativity and confusion and fear as essential human elements, paralyzing the future as well as the present.

Such an insightful analysis!

But does this mean that true gentleness contains an element of negativity? It does, indeed, and therein lies the crux of the problem: gentleness has its own dialectic. Not the dialectic that crushes, but the dialectic that plays all the nuances of the gentle against each other, nuances that can fade all the way to black. For if caress, erotic games, children's bodies, fur, cats' bellies . . . are soft and gentle, the renunciation of the dying person who lets go is also gentle. There is gentleness in the farewell to life, in the "disconnection, the illusion of total disconnection," in abandonment, in bereavement, in renunciation.

One would like to be able to present here all the artistic references that support the philosophical pictoriality. Literature, Tolstoy, Melville, Hugo (a wonderful reading of *The Man Who Laughs*), cinema (*Dolce Vita*), painting itself (Rembrandt, Giotto). . . . Each tableau is a surprise and a celebration, of the mind and the senses ("as if our senses were raw").

What then do we know at the end of this inexhaustible journey about what gentleness *is*—for this was the question. . . . Well, gentleness is not exactly kindness, it's not exactly the good, it's not exactly generosity, it's not exactly the taste of sugar (sweet), it's not exactly the quality of velvet, it's not exactly a low-intensity sound (quiet music, soft pedal), it's not exactly the clandestine (leaving on the sly). It is all of this simultaneously without being any one of these elements more than the other.

This notional shimmering is equal to its ambition. *Power of Gentleness* is an important text that teaches us, comforts us, disturbs us, too, that in any case *touches* us, always, at every moment. From this book that is so devoted to fragility, the reader emerges—and this is incontestable—that much stronger.

TRANSLATORS' NOTE

The paradox at the heart of Anne Dufourmantelle's collection of meditations is immediately apparent to French readers in her title *Puissance de la douceur*. *Puissance* is most often translated as *power*, as we have translated it, but it can also mean *strength* or *might*, even sometimes having a divine, royal, or military connotation. Dufourmantelle is interested in examining these micro-experiences of power, strength, and might in our everyday lives. But she is also interested in a *puissance* that refers to Aristotle's idea of potentiality—the power to change, or the potential of a possible future. All these connotations are implied when she pairs *puissance* with *douceur*.

Douceur is often translated as *gentleness*, but can also be translated as sweetness or softness. It can refer to the sweetness of sugar and treats (*une petite douceur*), or it can be used to describe a person's overall agreeable disposition, as in being nice or doing something sweetly.

The French *doux or douce* also describes objects that are silky, soft, smooth in texture, or delicate in nature. To do something *doucement* means to do it slowly, carefully, or gingerly. Along with wishing someone a *bon voyage* you might also wish someone an *atterrissage en douceur* (soft landing). *Douceur* is the word that connotes ease in movement, smooth transitions, graceful beginnings, and a soft touch. The word *gentleness* shares many of these qualities but certainly not all. *Gentleness* is a bit closer to *kindness* and *generosity* than *douceur* is; however, we chose it in consultation with the author not only because it worked well in so many of *douceur*'s contexts, but also because gentleness harmonizes with Dufourmantelle's project of a hospitable *douceur*, an absolute gift in the selfless sense inspired by Derrida's definitions of hospitality and forgiveness. In Dufourmantelle's prose, the repeated use of *douceur* echoes throughout the book, reminding us of the word's varied and multifaceted connotations that, along with *puissance*, are explored in all their polysemy.

In almost all cases, we choose to translate *douceur* and its adjectival form *doux/douce* as *gentleness* and *gentle*, and *puissance* as *power*. However, if context calls for a different connotation, we use a word that more accurately conveys that particular meaning and indicates the change with the original word in brackets [*douceur*] or [*puissance*]. For instance, when we learn that there is power *in the becoming*, we use *potentiality*. We choose *sweetness* or *softness* for certain sensory images of *douceur* that are specific to taste and texture. Also, in the chapter "Clandestine Gentleness," Dufourmantelle revels in the rich, ambiguous possibilities of the idiom *en douce*, meaning *on the sly*. In one sentence *en douce* refers to doing something discreetly, while in another sentence *en douce* refers to doing something softly, and in yet another instance it refers to poignant secrecy. Because each instance of *en douce* in this chapter explores a unique image or usage of the idiom, we translate each instance of *en douce* in a way that conveys the meaning of that particular image or usage and indicate [*en douce*] in brackets. This decision was made with careful deliberation and in conversation with Dufourmantelle.

Within the book Dufourmantelle also reconnects *douceur* to its etymological and cultural histories (such as martial arts, equestrian arts, Ancient Greek conceptions of heroism and hospitality) in which the paradox of power and gentleness is at play. This reconnection to the past allows us as readers to envision a present and future that could be replete with this powerful gentleness that Dufourmantelle describes. Within the etymologies and connotations of the French *douceur*, Dufourmantelle reinforces two related English words that convey many of the qualities of *douceur*: *meekness* and *fairness*. Dufourmantelle takes the time to explain these English concepts to her French audiences, and we have preserved these explanations, hoping that readers will recognize that the fully nuanced meaning of *douceur* or *gentleness* might disappear from one context but just as slyly reappear in a different, unexpected context. For English-language readers it is also worth noting that *douceur* has become an English word spelled the same way as the French, although the English *douceur* has migrated far from its seventeenth-century French origins. In English *douceur* is a bribe or tip, something given to "sweeten" a transaction. In this change from one language to another, and from one generational understanding of the concept to a different generational understanding, lies Dufourmantelle's underlying point: that generations of culture have morphed or witnessed the metamorphosis of this concept to the extent that we have detached ourselves from its full potential, and perhaps from our own human potential.

In translating this book, it also became important for us to convey nuances and paradoxes with a sense of poetry. Dufourmantelle's style is marked by short chapters, section breaks, and sentence fragments. This style conveys open space—on the page and in one's mind—in which to consider Dufourmantelle's vision. Dufourmantelle's sentence fragments also convey a pared-down focus on the essential, a voice that is comfortably asserting itself while questioning and undermining prevailing notions of power, weakness, sensory experience, and connection. For this reason, we chose to preserve Dufourmantelle's sentence fragments and sometimes unconventional word choices. If a particular image was unclear, we consulted Dufourmantelle about the translation and sought her clarification and approval.

Moreover, the poetic sentence fragments offer unexpected and interconnected images rather than simple dialectical argument. This is most obvious in moments such as, "Hills of low grass and barren rose bushes in the winter light." These moments offer sensory experience while reinforcing Dufourmantelle's carefully formed ideas about gentleness and light, gentleness and the bloom and decay of life, etc. Her unusual sensory details often draw novel connections between ideas, people, and objects, for example, "Cinnamon, amber and something else; no one is unaffected by that memory. You think of all the possible lives suddenly made present by a fragrance." In an instant, lives are "made present," and we participate in the "Sensory Celebration" that is woven into each of these chapters.

The fact that there is no exact equivalent for the French *douceur*, not in the English *douceur* and not even in *gentleness*, suggests that as an English-language culture we may be missing some of the far-reaching effects of the concept as well as its embedded *puissance*—the power and potentiality that Anne Dufourmantelle insists upon. This translation, then, has the double possibility of portraying Dufourmantelle's ideas and expanding and deepening philosophical understandings of certain words like *power*, *gentleness*, and *listening*. Our hope is that English-language readers will have an expansive view of the concept of gentleness, begin to see it where they have never seen it before, and begin to appreciate it as power when it occurs.

In the true spirit of gentleness, we would like to thank Catherine Porter for her ongoing dedication to translation and for her friendship, which was the genesis of our introduction to this project. We would also like to thank Fordham University Press and our publisher, Thomas Lay, for their dedication in making this book a reality. A heartfelt thank-you also goes to the French Voices program for their support and encouragement. We also owe a huge debt of gratitude to Elizabeth Rottenberg, who vetted the translation and offered helpful feedback and suggestions through every step of the process. Her input and advice were invaluable. And finally, to the inimitable Anne Dufourmantelle for bringing these ideas to life and patiently addressing our questions about the translation. She oversaw the completion of this translation, going so far as to suggest the cover art and the book's now uncanny subtitle, but passed away in July 2017 before it was printed.

POWER OF GENTLENESS

INTRODUCTION

Gentleness is invincible

—MARCUS AURELIUS

Gentleness is an enigma. Taken up in a double movement of welcoming and giving, it appears on the threshold of passages signed off by birth and death. Because it has its degrees of intensity, because it is a symbolic force, and because it has a transformative ability over things and beings, it is a power.

A person, a stone, a thought, a gesture, a color . . . can demonstrate gentleness. How do we approach such singularity? Approaching it is risky for those who want to comprehend it. In many ways it has the fierce nobility of a wild beast. The same could be said of a few other rare species: innocence, courage, astonishment, vulnerability.

Existing in the margin of concepts patrolled by the grand history of thought, they are watched by philosophy with an anxious eye. They require an unprecedented flexibility because they do not let themselves be defined only in terms of value, nor do they let themselves be contained in the description of their phenomenon.

We might limit ourselves to situating gentleness on a sensitivity frequency, recording its magnitude. But the intention behind it then disappears, reducing it merely to a kind of mood. Who senses "the gentleness" of an act, of a thought, of an object? Its recipient? The one who grants it? Does it occur without witness or author? Calm, delight, tact are spiritual benefits as well as physical. This is one of the many paradoxes of the concept that seems to float in the spheres of the ideal: it manifests its power only because it is also profoundly sensual.

Gentleness incites violence because it doesn't offer any possible foothold on authority. Dostoyevsky, Melville, Hugo, Flaubert, or the Tolstoy of "Master and Man" utilize it as the elusive force that opposes injustice. So much so that those who embody gentleness are condemned in the eyes of men. From Prince Myshkin[1] to the vagrants of Hamsun,[2] those called the innocents do not know they carry a gentleness that destines them to wandering and loneliness. Its contiguity with goodness and beauty makes it dangerous to a society that is never more threatened than when there exists a relationship between an individual and the absolute.

In the symbolic order as in certain martial arts, gentleness can drive back and defeat evil better than any other response. Nothing can force it or commit others to it. In our day, gentleness is sold to us under its diluted form of mawkishness. By infantilizing it our era denies it. This is how we try to overcome the high demands of its subtlety—no longer by fighting it, but by enfeebling it. Language itself is therefore perverted: what our society intends for the human beings that it crushes "gently," it does in the name of the highest values: happiness, truth, security.

If love and joy have essential affinities with gentleness, is it because childhood holds the enigma? Gentleness shares with childhood a kind of natural community but also a power. It is the secret lining, or where the imaginary joins the real in a space that contains its own secret, making us feel an astonishment from which we can never entirely return.

APPROACH

I have often asked myself and never found an answer
whence kindness and gentleness come,
I don't know it to this day, and now must go myself.
—GOTTFRIED BENN

In Latin *dulcis* signifies all possible gentlenesses, and *suavitas* describes God himself. Rhenish mysticism goes so far as to find an incomparable gentleness in nothingness. But philosophy doesn't treat gentleness this way; neither a concept nor merely a custom, it requires recognition but does not bend to judgment. Its apparent simplicity is misleading. And yet its singularity has always been confirmed. It is an active passivity that may become an extraordinary force of symbolic resistance and, as such, become central to both ethics and politics. It is also a way of life that has required development over millennia. Refinement has admittedly come from cruelty as well as from gentleness. No culture has acquired one without pursuing the other.

Gentleness is troubling. We desire it, but it is inadmissible. When they are not despised, the gentle are persecuted or sanctified. We abandon them because gentleness as power shows us the reality of our own weakness. Literature has given us memorable figures, notably Billy Budd, the servant of "A Simple Heart," the young Mohune,[3] and so many others; most end in an asylum, in prison, or dead. The strangeness of their gentleness creates a scandal.

How can the lack of gentleness in existence, in memory, and in the fragility of beings be heard? This lack is barely audible; I don't even know if it is truly perceived. It arises by default within an increasingly present norm imposed by a society claiming to be democratic and liberal but whose consumerist logic makes beings indistinguishable within an economy that tolerates no qualms.

Gentleness is a force of secret life-giving transformation linked to what the ancients called "potentiality" [*puissance*]. Without it there is no possibility for life to advance in its becoming. I think that the power of life's metamorphosis is sustained in gentleness. When the embryo becomes a newborn, when the cocoon blossoms into a butterfly, when a simple stone becomes the stele of a sacred space in the gardens of Kyoto, there is, at the very least, gentleness. From listening to those who come to me and confide their despair, I have heard it expressed in each personal experience. I have felt its force of resistance and its intangible magic in the secret of what is called "transference." But I undoubtedly perceived it as a child in the tangible relationship to all things.

Gentleness summons the body, that is to say, the idea of a body that gentleness would embody and disembody at the same time. We can imagine that brutality is dissolved on contact with the uterine water protecting the baby, but not always. Gentleness does not belong only to the human race. It is a quality whose infinite range extends beyond the realm of the living.

ORIGINS

Life places gentleness within us originally. We would think to grasp it from the source—a child sleeping soundly, the sweet taste of its mother's breast milk, voices that soothe, chant, caress—we guess it to be elsewhere, in the movement of an animal, the rise of darkness in the summer, the truce of a battle, the meeting of a gaze. We recognize it from the bedside of the dying, their gaze that calmly passes through their feverless agony, but even there it won't let itself be grasped. It comes to calm the fever of lovers and to oppose the executioner with a final breath, against which he can do nothing.

We perform acts of gentleness. We demonstrate gentleness. We soften the end of a life, its beginning. Gentleness is an enigma in its simplicity. It comes to recognize its own obviousness. As giver and receiver, it belongs just as much to touch as to thought.

Is it originally a quality of being? An experience? An ethic? A lie? Is there a primitive sensoriality that might have located gentleness one day?

Coming from further than living memory, there where mother and child are one, bodies merged, gentleness evokes a lost paradise. An original *before* that might be a dawn. But from the beginning there will already have been violence, terror, murder. Mimicry and competition that enflame hatred; no speech without betrayal and no civilization without an appeal to the most refined cruelty. Paradise is always already lost as it is measured against the origin, and this observation does not belong only to the melancholy. Living is a conquest wrenched from this passion of loss, a passion that is also an illusion reminiscent of epics, narratives, myths. We must have the courage to not consent to this lost paradise because it is a terrible mistake; it will open the door to all future resentments. It will justify the sacrifice.

Gentleness also comes *after* the separation and the searing pain of that first breath, after the hunger, after the anxiety, after the cry.

Disturbing, pacifying, dangerous, it appears on the edge. On the other side, once across the threshold. Of empty, of full, of space, of time, of heaven, of earth, it intrudes between signs, between life and death, between the beginning and the end. Indistinguishable from the range of feelings it accompanies—kindness, protection, compassion. It is bordered because it offers itself as a passage. In diffusing itself it alters. In indulging itself it metamorphoses. It opens in time a quality of presence within the tangible world.

Gentleness invents an expanded present. We talk about gentleness, acknowledging it, delivering it, collecting it, hoping for it. It is the name of an emotion of which we have lost the name, coming from a time when humanity was not dissociated from the elements, from animals, from light, from spirits. At what point did the human race become aware of it? What was gentleness opposed to when life and survival were merged?

ANIMALITY

Of animality, gentleness keeps the secret. A fundamental and paradoxical wildness, as foreign to any kind of taming as childhood. Not falling only under the human condition, it delineates its limits. So close to animality that it sometimes merges with it, gentleness is experienced to the point of making possible the hypothesis of an instinct that it would call its own. It would be the trait of a primal "gentleness drive" of protection, of compassion—even of goodness itself. An instinct closest to the being that would be devoted not only to self-preservation but also relationships.

What the animal disarms in advance, even in its cruelty (outside the range of human barbarity), is our duplicity. The human subject is divided, exilic. If the animal's gentleness affects us in this way, it is undoubtedly because it comes to us from a being that coincides with itself almost entirely.

TAKING CARE

In the beginning animals and humans go through the same stages. Without care, does a newborn survive? Doesn't it need to be protected, surrounded, spoken to, thought of, or imagined so it can truly *enter* the world? What does it become with an absolute lack of gentleness? A mother's care of the small mammal is another expression of the envelopment of what has not yet finished growing and finds itself threatened in its integrity. The study of early attachment indicates that the baby's body, like that of the animal, retains in memory all the intensities (and all the deficiencies) that have been lavished upon it. Any serious attack will endanger, now or later, its capacity to survive.

American philosophers have named this thought "care" because it allowed them to speak of the vulnerability of beings in a groundbreaking way. Taking the appropriate actions to curb the disease, close up the wound, alleviate the pain: from the beginning of humanity care has been related to gentleness. It expresses the good intention beyond what is given, beyond the medical act or the analgesic substance. Those who work with very premature babies know this, because the mysterious survival of those babies, who are fragile but also have astonishing resilience, may be due to the fact that a word, an act, have been given with tenderness. Is gentleness sufficient to heal? It equips itself with no power, no knowledge. Embracing the other's vulnerability means that the subjects cannot avoid recognizing his own fragility. This acceptance is a force; it makes gentleness a higher degree of compassion than simple care. To empathize, to "suffer with" is to experience with the other what he feels, without giving in to it. It means being able to open yourself up to others, their grief or suffering, and to contain that pain by carrying it elsewhere.

But gentleness is not only a principle of relation, regardless of the intensity behind it. It makes way for what is most singular in others. If the attention of gentleness, in the sense intended by Patočka as "care for the soul,"[4] beckons to our responsibility as human beings toward the world around us, toward the beings making up this world and even toward the thoughts we commit to it, then gentleness is part of an intimate connection to animality, to the mineral, the vegetal, the stellar.

INTELLIGENCE

Gentleness is primarily an intelligence, one that carries life, that saves and enhances it. Because it demonstrates a relationship to the world that sublimates astonishment, possible violence, capture, and pure compliance out of fear, it may alter everything and every being. It is an understanding of the relationship with the other, and tenderness is the epitome of this relationship.

Philosophy is suspicious of emotions. For a long time they were a single factor of obfuscation or bewilderment of reason. Only thought could decant the intelligible from the sensible. And require us to consider wisdom outside the dominion of affection, of the body and of sensitive moods. Asking the tools of reason to apply themselves to gentleness is an intrusion by one order of knowledge into another that eschews precisely that order. Yet what it summons us to is essential: thinking of the value of what alters us "for the better," and what distributes itself in the form of conscience. Because it implies a relation of the subject to otherness, its quality does not only designate the substance or the atmosphere that it delivers but that which, in itself, establishes connections: "*intelligere*." Its privilege is agreement. It takes into account cruelty, the injustice of the world. Being gentle with objects and beings means understanding them in their insufficiency, their precariousness, their immaturity, their stupidity. It means not wanting to add to suffering, to exclusion, to cruelty and inventing space for a sensitive humanity, for a relation to the other that accepts his weakness or how he could disappoint us. And this profound understanding engages a truth.

We can't help but observe violence, fanaticism, brutality, cynicism; they reign within servility as much as they do within authority, and they continue to be exercised for all purposes. But if gentleness can have the intelligence to comprehend violence, sometimes including it in its inevitability or because it recognizes its history, then the reverse is not true. And there will always be nobility in gentle power—without condemnation, reexamining what devastates and what is devastated by violence.

There is an art that further illustrates the inherent intelligence of gentleness: the equestrian art. It requires agreement between human and animal to a high degree of refinement and complicity. One must comprehend (guess, tolerate) the other to the point of being accepted by him. The horse may be guided, trained, bridled, whipped, but it will accommodate the rider only if the latter knows how to gently find the lightness of hand and the movement that will adjust to the stride of the animal. There is in the equestrian an art of gentleness like no other. Its mastery has a history as long as that of the domestication of the horse; it has required centuries in order to find its rules, its value, its ethics. And this agreement is not given once and for all; it plays itself anew each time.

POTENTIAL

Certain things are destined to happen according to a principle intrinsic to their nature. They will be called: *potential* [*en puissance*]. They carry a process dormant in its own becoming. Present in the most intimate of the living, they are a germination (*dynamis* in Greek) whose expansion also pertains to time itself. The sine qua non condition of the expression of this possible persistence of the living. The movement of life is to bloom or decay, there is no indeterminacy. Only idea accepts neutrality, but in time and reality, there is growth or decline (unbinding, Freud would say).

Aristotle identified power as the ability of a being to grow into his becoming.[5] A seed contains a "potential" [*en puissance*] tree, although in its material reality nothing would allow us to detect it. It is an endogenous concept that finds in its process both its limit (we will not be able to make this kernel become a rose or an umbrella) and its fulfillment (the willow "realizes" the seed completely). Gentleness as power determines the ripening of what is until then idle within the thing itself. When the embryo develops, it "breathes" the amniotic fluid until the ninth month of gestation. Its lungs are still awaiting activation. And it is still very difficult for embryotic development specialists to understand how, and by what signal, this *potential* [*en puissance*] pulmonary respiration manages to be realized. We can be seized with vertigo before the complexity of the mechanics of the neurobiological signals necessary for this purpose and nevertheless be dazzled by the simplicity and the evidence with which the first cry of the newborn signals the metamorphosis. The same fundamental question arises for the embryologists with stem cells or in the case of the lungs: how does the cell "know" what it needs to perform? What the Ancients outlined in this way: at what moment is the soul "given form," at what moment does it breathe into matter? Does the soul that contemplates perfect forms have in memory—a token of reminiscence—the idea of gentleness? The question remains unresolved.

This force of metamorphosis will be approached by philosophers in several ways. The ontological foundation that Spinoza offers is that of *conatus*,[6] in other words, the effort to persist in being. Nietzsche rejects this hypothesis while sketching the very essence of this concept in *Will to Power*. He considers that it is "the really fundamental instinct of life which aims at the expansion of power and, wishing for that, frequently risks and even sacrifices self-preservation."[7] Even more so than the perseverance of being by Spinoza's *conatus*, the Nietzschean will to power seems to be the antithesis of gentleness. Its contrary expression: force, intensified outpouring of life and metamorphosis of becoming into acquiescence to that same becoming. In support of that in *Ecce Homo*, Nietzsche poses gentleness as a formidable force of resistance to power. An ambivalent force born of a world sick with weakness, but a force stranger yet than any weakness. Gentleness is at times a decantation that requires in its essence an immense amount of accumulated, contained, and sublimated energy until it becomes immaterial. In this it may be an activation of the sensitive within the intelligible. Without it, would there be a possible passage between these orders?

THE SENSORY CELEBRATION (I)

Nothing but stillness can remain when hearts are full
Of their own sweetness, bodies of their loveliness.
—W. B. YEATS

Gentleness is an occasion for sensory celebration. Tact and the tactile, touch, taste, perfumes, sounds, all opening access. If it can instill violence in fragility, be beautiful, erotic, enter into a sacred dance with the desired body of the other, it is not without secret. That is to say, without freedom until the last moment.

Gentleness has many affinities to light. Its radiation, its intensity, its transformations, its night. If it had to be pictured in space it would be a moving curve, however miniscule. Music being the most direct translation perhaps, along with touch. The contrasting melodic lines harmonize with the rhythm, the voice, and the instrument. The andantes of Mozart's 21st and 24th concertos are not only perfect, they weave a cathedral of sounds. A perfect balance. In the music of the Renaissance and of the Middle Ages we actually hear the sacred and sensitive tessitura. When Anne Azema sings the *lais* of the troubadours or the lament of Isolde, gentleness is elevated to its most passionate.

The image is another entrance into gentleness. The painting *The Return of the Prodigal Son* by Rembrandt at the Hermitage in Saint Petersburg is a wonderful example of this.

Tact, the intelligence of touch, is an accelerator of life that halts madness. During psychotic episodes gentleness is frightening. It is the mortal disparity between the real and its shadow projected within the psyche. Each sensation foretells a possible danger.

Refinement coincides with gentleness, particularly in craftsmanship. It is the way wood is carved, worked, the subtlety of its color, the unfolding of a curve in the late Baroque period. Gentleness seems to be inlaid with the gesture, joined to it within the material. Five thousand coats of lacquer were required in order to make a piece of furniture for the royal court in Beijing. In accounts, the touch was said to have been like the gentleness of rain and the fineness of a child's hair. The softness [*douceur*] of silk, polished glass, spun silver, the texture of velvet, of the skin that it covers, of the eye beholding them.

Hieratic figures made by Giotto. The illuminated fixed in a simplicity that gives them, like that of the convent cells painted by Fra Angelico, a sweetness without weakness or mannerism. Their gentleness invites the viewer to participate in a scene that cannot help but ensure distance. It holds at bay the gaze where it alights.

Gentleness joining sky and sea in Venice. Gentleness of summer skies, of atmospheres, of clouds. Delicacy in these non-closed edges—interior and exterior, liquid and ethereal.

Gentleness of lamps at night. The halo and its limitation. Their preciseness, often on stage. Cutting a naked body. The cutout of an alcove. The high flame. All these edges of light that darkness defines and in a way protects.

There is no limit to gentleness, rather a continual invitation to become infected by it—and that invitation can be broken in an instant.

The values that agree with gentleness are sometimes grueling, they require an etiquette above and beyond what is encouraged as a mere sweetener to our lives. They require keeping watch.

Is gentleness only obvious when it deserts us, and when it returns? When suffering ends, when the rolling of the wave leaves foam on the sand as gentle as air, or is it rather a singular essence savored only for its own sake?

An animal's belly. The throbbing of a vein that surfaces from under the skin. Very aged skin like a translucent pebble. The skin of a very young child, his or her cheek still covered in an invisible fuzz. The calm of breathing, of what contains and protects life. And of what offers itself through touch.

Gentleness is also harmony. The manner in which the orchestra harmonizes, or in which two of Rothko's flat planes will interact along a red horizon. It is the proportion of a face.

The sweetness of the ineffable. Beauty of what doesn't appear in the given appearance of things and phenomena, of what can only be touched in a face, of what loosens its grip entirely. Gentleness reveals the gap between what is there and what escapes. The carnal and the spiritual, but not only the gaps, the ellipses—in language, in the visible, in the baroque spiral, in the lines of anamorphosis.

SALES PITCH

Gentleness sells. It is set before us in all its forms, everywhere, constantly. It is an economic argument paid to the
account of what has nothing to do with it. The absolute
lack of consideration for beings that the neoliberal world
reveals in the power relations established as secret norms
in the workplace, at school, and even in leisure activities
is carried out today, and this is new, under the cover of
safety requirements and by being careful to resort to
the so-called demands of the subjects themselves: voluntary servitude is a program that runs smoothly. Therefore, it is not surprising that gentleness is used as an
excuse to ennoble objects of consumption, or that we as-
sociate it with laundry detergent, sweets, and even busi-
ness advice. But it is also summoned most ominously in
areas of pure constraint, or even extortion. Because we
are in a moment of history where perversion proves its
worth and where its recurring and contaminating power

is increasingly virulent. It will exercise itself precisely in the name of gentleness. To pervert a meaning is to turn it into its opposite under the guise of serving or admiring it. It is above all the twisting of language and mind that we are made to believe is necessary.

Gentleness is also divided in two by bodies of socioeconomic control. On the carnal side, it is bastardized into silliness. On the spiritual side, into New Age potion and other methods competing to make us believe that it is enough to believe in them in order for everything to work. Theories of self-improvement and pursuit of happiness participate in spite of themselves in this grand marketplace of "well-being" that refuses to enter into negativity and confusion and fear as essential human elements, paralyzing the future as well as the present. This division is in its essence formidable because it assaults the connection that gentleness establishes between the intelligible and the sensible.

We are in a moment in history—this tone may be a bit too solemn for my taste, but how else can I say it?— where manipulation techniques are proving themselves. Their effectiveness no longer needs to be proven; they are in a certain way guarantors of their own effectiveness. Rather it is their power of reversal that is most insidious. The very fact that in the name of "gentleness" we come to justify brutality or any other falsification of this kind seems not only allowed today but also encouraged. It is to distill into a principle what will make it deny the very essence that constituted it. It is the judge who, with equanimity, assaults the child whom later that afternoon he will defend as innocent; it is the mother who scars this same childhood by "giving" herself as a sacrifice; and the list goes on sounding almost outmoded because the infiltration of that mode of reversal is subtle, relentless, and alert. There is no need for an all-seeing "big eye"[8] that we could attack or even suspect, it is all of us who have entered the factory. And we are simultaneously the victims and the instigators.

Gentleness will be the name by which violence is performed. Barbarism. The worst meanness will be an elevation. By technological intrusion, we have entered an era of denials and reversals. Yet I believe that gentleness resists. Resists perversion. As before and after it, madness resisted; but madness abandons human interaction with the so-called real world. Gentleness doesn't.

LANGUAGE SOURCES

At this point, it is time to examine language. When we forget etymology it is not merely a question of lack of culture, but a question of relation to the collective memory. It is to be unaware that the misappropriations, the erasures, the substitutions of meaning are also the instruments of political and societal censorship. It is not a matter of rehabilitating a "pure" language. All purity, as we know, is questionable—this is the first place that perversion will attack. Returning to the way Ancient Greece conceived of and named gentleness, it is the very relation that a human community maintains with the law, justice, war, but also with the so-called values of the "heart" that emerges. And with it, that which we call humanism. For the Greeks, gentleness is the opposite of *hubris*, the opposite of this excessiveness that takes hold of humans in the throes of what we call today their "drives," but neither is it moral rigor; no, in a certain way gentleness belongs more to the gods than to humans. Although it is tangible just as much as it is intelligible, it comprises the good without being the good, the relationship without being a relationship, the spiritual without being a divine attribute, or matter in its pure receptivity.

There are two words for gentleness in Greek: *proates*, meaning gentleness, kindness. In the Epistles, Saint Paul thus evokes "a spirit of gentleness" necessary for the establishment of a community.[9] From the outset, gentleness involves the question of "being together," the close circle of politics and ethics. But *praos* also means gentleness, a more sensibility-laden term meaning good-natured that the Vulgate will translate into Latin as *mites* (in English, "meek"—"poor and gentle"). In the Beatitudes we find, "Blessed are the meek for they shall inherit the earth."[10] *Mites* for a fruit means that it is ripe and tender; *mites* for the earth, fertility; for a being, gentleness and goodness. In Latin two other words express gentleness: "*suavitas*,"—more intellectual or spiritual, and "*dulcis*,"—that gave melodiousness (to a sound), attractiveness, beauty (to a thing), and sweetness (to food). With the advent of Christianity, the awaited king/messiah in all his splendor is replaced by a child born in poverty and exile. Placing spiritual royalty in the place of the greatest vulnerability was a coup de force unprecedented in History. All the values of merit, of power, and of military prowess found themselves disrupted.

Greek Antiquity, centered on the values of heroism, justice, and questions governing public life, seems foreign to the "sentimental" virtues: *The Iliad* is a poem of conquests, trickery, and death. In her excellent book,[11] Jacqueline de Romilly shows how in Homer, certain words appear that underscore courtesy and persuasion as opposed to violence. It is about extending the idea of justice in the form of clemency, restraining the hand of vengeance. Homer makes it appear where it seems the least expected. When King Priam asks Achilles for the body of his son Hector, murderer of Achilles' best friend, Achilles agrees, has the body of the deceased washed, and receives Priam at his table. He requests that the battle be suspended long enough for the old king to bring his son back to Troy. The Homeric heroes are the most passionate and therefore most capable of gentleness *out of respect*. Their gentleness does not indulge in any sentimentality, and it harmonizes with courage.

Values of intimacy in the Greek world were the sole prerogative of the gods. Their passions, their betrayals, their moods were commented on by the people who suffered the unfair consequences. In Aeschylus's theater, the most monstrous goddesses, the furies, finally agree to integrate themselves into a world where a just god, capable of bringing healing, reigns; they assume the name of *Eumenides* or "Kindly Ones."[12]

At this point the word *philanthrōpos* appears and leads us further down the path of an attitude of indulgent kindness. It no longer denotes only an external process or way of acting but a universal disposition; an active solidarity irrespective of the circumstances. It expresses a feeling of community before human fragility, like the feeling of Ulysses before the madness of Ajax:

> I know none nobler; and I pity him
> In his misery, albeit he is my foe,
> Since he is yoked fast to an evil doom.
> My own lot I regard no less than his.
> For I see well, naught else are we but mere
> Phantoms, all we that live, mere fleeting shadows.[13]

The imperfection of human nature, considered for a long time to be a fault or an excuse, became a source of pity and brotherhood. Plato uses it in *The Symposium* concerning love when he has Aristophanes say, "Of all the gods [*philanthrōpo*] is the best friend of men"[14] and has him claim that it will be an art that will aid humanity. Thus we invoke his philanthropy when we talk of Socrates's generosity, whose teaching was free. But in Greece this notion of philanthropy remains a question of equity and does not go so far as sacrifice,

Christian abnegation: "Gentleness could not be able to prevail against justice and the reciprocity that it requires."[15]

After that, little by little, gentleness will depart from its relationship to force, to courage, and it will attempt to participate in the fleshless evanescence of a world promised to the ascetic ideal of a life devoted to the Most High. Severed from the flesh, gentleness then becomes lifeless and joins the exaltation of weakness.

JUSTICE AND FORGIVENESS

In short, for the philosophers, gentleness merges with civilization. And yet Plato struggles with indulgence; instead his thought is centered on justice and truth: "For equity (*epieikes*) and indulgence (*suggnomon*) are infractions of the perfect and strict rule of justice."[16] Even if, according to Socrates, "The unrighteous and vicious are always to be pitied in any case; and one can afford to forgive as well as pity him who is curable."[17] The difficulty for the Greeks is to achieve gentleness or *sophrosyne* (moderation) without conflicting with the values of courage, resolve, and the aptitude for war necessary within any political community. *Fairness*,[18] untranslatable into French, conveys that mixture of equity and gentleness. Aristotle, in *Nicomachean Ethics*, writes, "For the good-tempered [*doux*] man is not revengeful, but rather tends to make allowances."[19] With *suggnomé*, gentleness takes a unique inflection, denoting the possibility to remove an offense between humans and not just an offense from the gods toward humans. The capacity to forgive spreads in Greek thought. Derrida sheds light on this paradox of forgiveness: it only makes sense in the face of what cannot, must not be erased nor ever forgotten. In that place only the gesture of "for-give-ness,"[20] to give beyond, has a universal reach and, by the same token, creates a scandal. Here the gentleness within forgiveness is not even mentioned, the paradox only appears in its extremism. Yet to forgive is an act that gives gentleness to the one who can bestow it as well as the one who receives it.

And as often happens with gentleness, there is a double gift that appears: the one who offers it and the one who receives it are both brought together. How many children wait for it their entire lives, how many lives wasted away for an utterance that has never come? Forgiveness is conditioned on gentleness. Without inner revolution forgiveness is merely wished for, it does not become real, it is disabled by pity, courage, abdication, or envy, it frees nothing and only deepens a gaping wound. For Derrida, forgiveness is directed toward the living, but it is (ultimately) for the dead. It is always offbeat, unbalanced, and asymmetrical. Forgiveness is a violent act. It promises to set right time itself.

It is Rome that marries gentleness to forgiveness in the human world. Whatever has the feature of clemency appears here; it becomes included in the legal texts regulating everyday life. *The Great Roman Civil War* notes that Caesar offers to negotiate using his *misericordia* (Latin for "mercy"), *clementia* (goddess of forgiveness and mercy), and *liberalitas* (the concept of giving freely). According to Plutarch, the notion of gentleness blossoms like an ideal of life. We find new words signifying the disposition to love or to cherish, for example, in *The Life of Solon*: "For the soul has a spring of affection within in; it is formed . . . to love."[21]

As for Christianity, it will be foreign to the standards that defined Greek thought: gentleness in its ethical dimensions and *philia* was of no value to the city or the state, not even to life here on earth. In late Medieval Latin, God up above the Dasein, even above the Sein, is acknowledged for being praised in that word of a particular music: *suavité*. "How sweet did it suddenly become to me to be without the delights of trifles!"[22] (Augustine). What the Rhineland mystics and even Meister Eckhart and Hildegard of Bingen will take up and amplify to the extreme.

The saints are figures of force and of gentleness. Able to be spiritual fighters to the point of martyrdom, they confronted authority and disseminated goodness. One of them, Saint Francis of Assisi, remains a figure apart from the others of the West. Son of a wealthy cloth merchant and a French mother and an enthusiast for a form of poetry similar to that of the troubadours, he was known for his prodigality. He was taken prisoner, and after a long illness, he fundamentally changed his life and devoted himself to caring for the lepers. He wrote in his Testament, "And when I left [the lepers] I discovered that what had seemed bitter to me was changed into sweetness in my soul and body. And shortly afterward I rose and left the world."[23] He repaid his father for everything and severed ties with him. Saint Francis of Assisi led the life of a penitent in practicing asceticism, and he became known for living in brotherhood with all living beings. Here forgiveness and justice are upheld by him whose gentleness turns a merciless war against injustice into sainthood. The proximity of this saintly figure's gentleness to the plant and animal kingdoms is rare in the West.

EAST

In Hebrew gentleness is expressed as "*ʾǝnavah*" and denotes one who is humble, low. The "*ʾǝnavouim* are bowed
down, oppressed. There is another word for material
gentleness—sweet fruit. It occurs in *The Song of Songs*
several times, but also in *Ecclesiastes*. Gentleness is an attribute of God before it becomes a human attribute. In
the *Bible* the discouraged human literally has his "spirit
broken," his plight is at once gentleness and poverty.

But we must go back to the Sanskrit root to find this
link between spiritual benevolence, physical gentleness,
and moderation of heart. The slow evolution of the
Vedic sacrifice corresponds to a collection of specific texts.
The *Samaveda Samhita* is a compilation of sung praises
intended for the Brahmin singer. It is the "Veda in the
medium of cantillation." "Veda," this gender-neutral
word, also signifies in Sanskrit "gentleness, graciousness,

welcoming and kind speech." The importance of sound must be emphasized in Vedic culture, which considers the Veda to be the result of the ancient sages echoing the original sound emitted by the regularity of cosmic movements. To this day the Vedic tradition is oral and transmits the word—Rigveda—from Teacher to student by a modulated chant endowed with an incantatory force. In the subsequent Indian texts, for example, in the eight stanzas dedicated to Krishna, we find an almost somnambulistic repetition of the word: "His lips are sweet, His face is sweet, His eyes are sweet, His smile is sweet. . . ."[24]

Svadhishthana is the name of the second chakra or the sacral chakra. In Sanscrit it signifies "gentleness"; its element is water and its sense, taste. It is situated above the sexual organs. On a physical level, it acts upon the genitals, the sacrum. On an emotional level, the appetite, sexuality, consciousness of self, creativity, procreation, joie de vivre—or, once it is fulfilled: jealousy, guilt, dependency. That is the chakra of our genetic inheritance. Here gentleness is just as spiritual as it is carnal. The Eastern world has everything to teach us about a certain relationship to gentleness without sentimentality. In a civilization where Eros was not stigmatized, there was no rivalry between moral courage and self-denying behavior. Gentleness was neither infantilized nor politicized; it was first an art of refinement.

A SILENT TRANSFORMATION

We must recognize the central role that Chinese culture gives to transitions, to invisible germinations, and to sentient life. In the West changes are recognized according to the criterion of events, which are quickly categorized. We are blind to the imperceptible. In a culture of results, the discontinuous is a mirage. Yet in each instant everything changes. But how has this happened? Do we still perceive the moment of the event when we linger over every detail of an emerging process? Gentleness is cut from the same cloth because it is not perceptible categorically, but only existentially. As sensation and as passage, or as power of metamorphosis.

François Jullien, in his wonderful book, shows how often "silent transformations"[25] constitute what European metaphysics has the most difficulty understanding, while in contrast, Chinese culture regards them with intelligence. Since the Greeks, the West has graduated borders, maintained separate orders, questioned limits. One proceeds by concept and not by intuition, much less by analysis of sensations. Melting snow is one example: how do we define it? Indeed, at the heart of their thinking stands the question of stable identity and not of mutating identity.

A floating world is troubling for the West, undoubtedly because the ineffable belongs to God alone and not to the real. Deleuze and Bergson are among the few thinkers who insist on the question of the becoming of concepts. Because European thought has had an obsession with fixity of being. For example, the questions of the beginning (if there is metamorphosis, nothing allows us to detect an originating instant) and of the end (the transition does not aim for the result as a goal), or—even more surprising—that of time, do not pose themselves as such in Chinese thought. Attentive to annals, to exact dating, Chinese culture nevertheless has never thematized "time" as an overall and unique concept.

In ancient Chinese texts, transformation is an attitude, a state of body and mind, a harmony based on the "natural" pattern of things that mature and flourish, interacting with their surroundings. The Taoist attitude endeavors "to utilize the developing potential at play over time as well as the capacity of self-deployment of the processes."[26] Here we find the idea of potentiality [*puissance*] in the Aristotelian sense, but where Aristotle questions the way in which the sensation of gentleness appears for a subject, in China, it is gentleness itself that contains the seeds of its opposite. A passage resulting in a change of nature. No scansion or disconnection.

FEELING AND SENSIBILITY

> The virtues are only set affections.
>
> —BERNARD DE CLAIRVAUX

Far from the military prowess of Ancient Greece, far from the fury of the Medieval theological debates, far from the banner of universal harmony that the Renaissance carried, our era has chosen to be *sentimental* and to give all authority to our errant thoughts. Since German Romanticism, which had found for it one of the most lofty definitions, feeling (*Stimmung*), quite often lost itself in an abyss of complacency. Counterfeits emerged with increasing speed, giving rise to a kind of culture made of predigested, prefabricated "love," full of clichés. In a market society, sensibility is undermined; it is of no use to buying and selling if it is not channeled and normalized.

Sensibility, the vector of our most contradictory emotions, is an agent of freedom. Because it originates in our most unique perceptual apparatus and links us to the multifaceted and evolving manner of the world, it always escapes social radars. Feelings themselves, known for how high they can carry us, suffer from being linked to representations and in this respect are indissolubly "affected" by the time period. Today the instruction manuals of social functioning are integrated, the scenarios defined. As for sensibility, it exerts itself. Without exercise, it fades or withers. The art of the senses is not a pure receptivity; it also depends on our free will.

Gentleness belongs to sensibility, whether or not it stimulates feelings. By feelings we are affected, by feelings we are moved. If gentleness is weakened until its sharp edges and ambiguity are dissolved, then the power from which it originates and that it actualizes will be in turn threatened.

"That is how you stand: facing me, softly [*dans la douceur*], in constant provocation, innocent, unfathomable,"[27] says the narrator of "The Atlantic Man," by Duras. The words are not linked together at random; softness [*douceur*] is face to face with provocation, and it has the enigma and impenetrability of what we call innocence. The highest point of gentleness is its possible erasure—and that is precisely what frightens us. In its intelligence and strength, it may be the highest expression of sensibility, and nevertheless in each moment it may disappear.

THE SYMBOLIC FORCE
OF GENTLENESS

The symbolic force of gentleness is an authority. The East has revered this spiritual authority earlier and more profoundly than the West. From the Zen practices of Hinduism to the writings about the Tao of Confucianism and the Shamanic rites of Eastern Siberia, gentleness is not perceived as a weakness.

Gandhi is one of the most emblematic figures of nonviolence because he was both a great resistance fighter—a warrior in a sense—and a spiritual leader. It is interesting—and surprising—to consider the spiritual leaders who inspired him because three, and not the least of them, are Westerners. The first is Tolstoy. Their relationship began with a letter that the young lawyer addressed to the Russian genius toward the end of the year 1909. He explained to him the injustices suffered by Indians after the enactment of an unjust law by the

English. He asked Tolstoy's permission to publish his famous "Letter to a Hindu." Tolstoy granted him the permission he sought, and an epistolary relationship ensued. The spiritual doctrine of Tolstoy is summarized as follows: "The Christian will not dispute with anyone, nor attack anyone, nor use violence against anyone. On the contrary, he will bear violence without opposing it. But by this very attitude to violence, he will not only himself be free, but will free the whole world from all external power."[28] Tolstoy preached the refusal to serve or obey bad government. Gandhi showed that he had retained this lesson, when to the detriment of General Smuts, he ordered Indians to challenge his authority through civil disobedience.

Gandhi had in Ruskin another Western spiritual teacher. During his time in Johannesburg, a friend lent him *Unto This Last*, by Ruskin. Gandhi started to read the book as soon as the train departed from Johannesburg to Durban, and he continued to read it all night. Ruskin preaches the dignity of manual labor, recommends living simply, and stresses the debilitating complications of the modern economic system. Under the influence of this text, Gandhi decided to change his life. He purchased a farm and settled there with his family and others, and the group set out to live in harmony with Ruskin's principles.

Thoreau is the third interlocutor of Mahatma. Could this thinker have imagined that a hundred years after his death he would have a significant influence on the freedom of hundreds of thousands of Indians? His key essay, "Civil Disobedience," stayed with Gandhi, who had already defined his own policy of passive resistance and called it "satyagraha," which means "attachment to the truth." The passage by Thoreau often cited by Gandhi was, "It is not desirable to cultivate a respect for the law, so much as for the right. The only obligation which I have a right to assume is to do at any time what I think right."[29] When Gandhi read these texts for the first time, he was in prison precisely for this reason.

These three thinkers opposed the force of arms and men with the force of spirit. Gandhi risked his life without ever risking the life of his opponent by trusting symbolic force. The naysayers of this symbolic force bring out its gentleness. This gentleness offers a stark contrast to the violence that it incites.

FREE FORM

We recognize gentleness in literary figures that turned everything around them upside down without meaning to. Prince Myshkin, the majority of characters in Kafka, in Melville, in the short stories of Tolstoy, little John Mohune in *Moonfleet*—this impossible community of characters, who arrive from nowhere and without ever abandoning an unparalleled gentleness, provoke violence and passion around them because their radicality is irrevocable, has no contempt. These characters who embody gentleness in literature reveal the appearances under which all compromises are concealed. They polarize the real around an unprecedented truth that is impossible to bear. Bartleby and the servant of "A Simple Heart" are such outlaws. Their gentleness does violence to a world where the rules of consensual servitude are the coordinates. An excess of this gentleness is dangerous. Better than any searchlight, it reveals faults, desire, manipulation, or conversely, goodness.

Gentleness does not belong only to the good. There is within it the possibility of being manipulated, even if we cannot disentangle ourselves from the feeling that it belongs to what is most alive in life. Lavishing it on others or receiving it, even simply recognizing it, fundamentally means acquiescing to it—do we yield to gentleness or do we provoke it? The answer may lead us toward the place that in times of war we call "the front." Gentleness is a formidable ethic because it has made a pact with the truth. It cannot betray unless it is falsified. The threat of death itself is not enough to ward it off. Gentleness is political. It does not bend; it grants no prolonging, no excuse. It is a verb: we perform acts of gentleness. It aligns with the present and concerns all the possibilities of the human. From animality it takes instinct; from childhood, enigma; from prayer, calming; from nature, unpredictability; from light, light.

PURE GENTLENESS?

Can we conceive of goodness, joy, giving, calm without their opposites? Would gentleness have any value if it didn't also include brutality? Chinese thought has primarily expressed this idea by showing, for example, that within the yin and yang symbol each principle necessarily includes a tiny dot signifying the inclusion of the opposing principle. If gentleness is a consistent link that goes well beyond circumstances and events and that addresses being, we could define brutality as what comes to threaten that link. If there is gentleness, that is to say, also tenderness and protection, then violence must be exercised in order to end it. In fact, without any opportunity for the individual to cross over to its opposite, does gentleness remain a choice? Doesn't it indulge in sacrificial duty or psychological impairment?

In defeating gentleness, violence just admits that this gentleness may not be fully received in this world. The literary figures of innocence are its tragic heroes. They are similar to those child martyrs whom we sometimes brutalize to death because they pit their unyielding gentleness against the murderous drive that their freedom awakens and unleashes. Billy Budd is a young sailor who leaves the ship called *The Rights of Man* and is forcibly conscripted to serve on the warship *HMS Bellipotent*. His beauty and his youth fascinate the crew. His speech is hindered; he stutters when he is emotional, and this vulnerability will cost him his life. Captain John Claggart, jealous of the affection surrounding the young man, seeks to harm him. He embarks on a plan to expose the mutinous preparations that he accuses Billy of instigating. In light of recent mutinies within the British fleet, the commander is forced to listen to these unbelievable accusations. Billy is confronted by Claggart and must justify his actions, but he stutters and is unable to explain himself. He then brutally hits Claggart, who dies instantly. Billy is sentenced to death by hanging by a court martial to which the commander can offer only his own helpless testimony. Billy blesses him before being hanged, which prevents mutiny. Billy Budd is gentle. He doesn't defend himself; when he kills Claggart he is under the influence of emotion in the face of injustice. His beauty and his strangeness make him a scapegoat, through the desire he arouses and the strange "goodness" he has displayed throughout the story. He is a grown child in a man's body.

Despite the compassion the commander has for him, Billy can only be condemned. The law overshadows the human and must be respected. Billy failed to listen to the wise advice of an old sailor, who, like a Tiresias figure, had warned him of the merciless cruelty of the world to which he belonged. Here gentleness is the other side of deadly violence. It leads to a double crime (the crime of Billy Budd and the crime against Billy Budd). As a possible face of holiness, it reveals and activates the demons of the Other to the point that neither pity nor punishment can entirely understand or destroy it.

In his novel *The Man Who Laughs*, Victor Hugo embodies gentleness not in a figure of innocence but in one of absolute fidelity. Constancy and dedication form the implied oath that Gwynplaine and Dea have vowed to each other, but this also applies when it comes to all vows, to themselves. The boy has promised not to falter regarding an ideal of justice, and Dea must lend support to him on this path, whatever the cost. This bifrontal fidelity is made of the same force, a power but also the same infinite delicacy of attention. "'I represent the humanity such as its masters have made it,' cried Hugo. Mankind has been mutilated. That which has been done to me has been done to it." Gwynplaine's famous speech in the House of Lords says it all: "So, you insult misery. Silence, Peers of England! Judges, listen to the plea. . . . Listen to me and I will tell you. Oh! Since you are powerful, be brotherly; *since you are great, be gentle*."[30] Gwynplaine's gentleness permeates even in his conception of ideal justice. Dea herself is a character of pure goodness, of innocence, while Gwynplaine is complex, torn between his impulses, his beliefs, and his fascination with what he discovers to be his nobility. In this book, a dazzling gentleness makes a dent in perversion and, as a type of engagement, proposes resistance through theater, through nobility of soul, and through the loving withdrawal out of the worldly life. Gwynplaine is an example of a sad clown whose intelligence, like that of Oliver Twist—another famous orphan child—, does not save him from cynicism. Dea's love, whose blind girl's wisdom won't protect her from death, is his alter ego. These two figures of brother and sister, as often in Hugo, testify to the exorbitant cost of the search for freedom and truth. One is not achieved at the price of the other.

Gentleness doesn't present itself only in Christlike features of voluntary servitude or only in exemplary fidelity to an ideal. In Flaubert's short story, the "Simple Heart" is a servant who embodies a sort of "hindered" gentleness that is almost backward and surely traumatic, a servant who strives—until her dying breath—to maintain the connection to beings that she is required to serve by order and by vocation to the point of self-denial and disregard for her own life. Flaubert sums up the short story in his correspondence: "The story of 'A Simple Heart' is simply the tale of a forgotten life, that of a poor country girl, devout but mystical, devoted without exaltation and soft-hearted as fresh bread. . . . None of this is ironic as you suppose it to be, but on the contrary, extremely serious and extremely sad."[31]

Here the servant is a universal figure representing the loss of one's self in the other to the point of abnegation. Her gentleness is no longer the disarming simplemindedness of the innocent in a guilty world, but instead the instrument of a somewhat stubborn foolishness that is swept away by a more adapted world. She cannot find anything except slavery and death in return. The person—in this case the servant of Flaubert—who knows nothing except how to sacrifice herself, doesn't develop this gentleness as an art or as a choice but primarily in order to avoid conflict or violence. Gentleness then is transformed, less into a shelter than into a form of confinement. It works on the side of renunciation, even of morbidity. Most often this "pure" gentleness finds its source in the areas of trauma. "Pure" gentleness cannot access what Freud defines as constitutive hatred of the subject, which normally gives the baby the strength it needs to access language and to differentiate itself from the parental sphere. For if aggression is the divisive instance, it also allows survival, lest everything return to the same dead end.

Gentleness, like foolishness, doesn't speak well.

PATROLLING

To attack gentleness is an unnamed crime that our era often commits in the name of its divinities: efficiency, speed, profitability. We try to make it desirable, exchangeable, institutionalizable, so that it does not upset everything. We kill gentleness with gentleness. We make it into a contaminated drug, the need for which is inculcated in us.

The Dostoyevsky of *The Brothers Karamazov* summons gentleness in the scene of "The Grand Inquisitor." The Inquisitor knows that no one can bear Christ's return; he will therefore take upon himself the decision to condemn. Christ never departs for a moment from his gentleness, and it is that alone that defeats the power and the certainty of the Inquisitor. It comes to convert the forces of mortification, opening another path to the truth other than terror. Humans do not want the freedom that you offer them, says the Grand Inquisitor to Christ; I, who am conscious of this, offer myself as a sacrifice to that freedom, depriving them of it and taking the full burden. Humans prefer servitude; they want to be guided and discharged from the exorbitant choice of their existence. We see here that Freud had read Dostoyevsky, for what else does the obsessional neurotic do if he doesn't avoid at all costs paying the price of a freedom that he does not want? As often in Dostoyevsky, it is on the edges of baseness, betrayal, violence that gentleness becomes revealing. The beings who lavish gentleness are suffused with it like a fever that contaminates their interlocutors far from their usual territories. In their incapacity to be in the world otherwise than in this failure appears an unprecedented relationship to freedom. Because gentleness appears first as a failure. It infringes all the rules of social etiquette. The beings who demonstrate it are sometimes resisters, but they do not carry on the fight where it usually takes place. They are elsewhere. As incapable of betraying as they are of betraying themselves, their power comes from an act that is always a way of being in the world. And the passion that arises from it comes from the emotion that only gentleness may liberate: it is another living.

SENSORY CELEBRATION (II)

> No one had the courage to define the typical element
> in pleasure, every sort of pleasure ("happiness") as the
> feeling of power.
>
> —FRIEDRICH NIETZSCHE

Laughing, singing, loving—are powerful Dyonisian acts,
expressions of an authentic life. Gentleness involves the
body, that is to say, the idea and the sensibility of a body
that gentleness could have educated, elevated, ennobled.
Its power distilled by the senses.

We cannot possess gentleness. We offer it hospitality.
It is there, as discreet and necessary and vital as a heartbeat. Its carnal power goes from sensuousness to the
lightest pressure of the hand; it is thought when it touches
and touched when it is intelligence.

Gentleness has no fixed location in the body, it is there from birth, there where we breathe, it accompanies dreams and joins in their secret revolt, it only reveals itself after the fact, in the impression it leaves upon sleep.

No event in this world is foreign to it because it bears the responsibility of the living. Without gentleness, no existence in the human world. No possible translation except violence.

Gentleness resembles a child's wish. That whispered promise: I will always be by your side.

Unrevealed, like the wings of butterflies coiled within their cocoon, gentleness inhabits every thought in the process of its sensorial becoming.

Its power distills itself in the senses. It is erotic in all possible ways. Because the intention containing it is a taming of savagery of humors and body that also allows for the negative, shadow and darkness are part of the states of the desiring body. No gentleness without desire transmuting itself into caress, into play, and not bending itself upon possession.

Gentleness is underneath, lurking. Under every observed object, just below the line, it's there under every touched thing, every word spoken, every gesture begun, like an instrumental melody that accompanies a sung tune.

Gentleness is experienced. Dreamlike, it substantially modifies what it affects. It does not leave us unscathed.

The gentleness of rising pleasure. Letting go in the certainty of love and eroticism when playing and touching and taking and giving oneself and imagining all harmonize.

Gentleness is one of the sources of eroticism; it may reach its most savage lands, its most liberated lands. Without it, there would be no more space laced with shadows and light, no more drawing near, no more letting go, no more play, no inventions, no mirages.

If gentleness were a gesture, it would be a caress.

The caress is like contact, is sensibility. But the caress transcends the sensible. It is not what it would feel beyond the felt, further than the senses, that it would seize upon a sublime food while maintaining, within its relation with this ultimate felt, an intention of hunger that goes unto the food promised, and given to, and deepening this hunger, as though the caress would be fed by its own hunger. The caress consists in seizing upon nothing, in soliciting what ceaselessly escapes its form toward a future never future enough, in soliciting what slips away as though it were not yet. It searches, it forages. It is not an intentionality of disclosure but of search: a movement unto the invisible.[32]

COUNTERFEITS

The opposite of gentleness is not brutality or violence itself, it is the counterfeit of gentleness: what perverts it by imitating it. All forms of compromise, diluted suavity, sentimental mush. All those slogans suavely but firmly prescribed by a society in dire need of harmony are dangerous counterfeits. More than brutality, they pervert its nature or rather its connection. Because gentleness establishes a connection to the world, to the other, to the principle of life itself—from which it originates.

Thanks to communion with the inferred world, we can experience a certain detachment that may confine us to a desert crossing—a path carried to its height by the mystics. Of these moments of loss where no more refuge is offered to us. This moment of darkness, or of nihilism, seems to be as distant as possible from gentleness, and yet it is precisely when all support is lost and when all hope is gone that its reversal can take place.

In today's age, it has become intolerable to "withdraw ourselves," or else this withdrawal must be announced, scheduled, and registered. The secret garden is identified by a sign, which means that it is no longer secret. Gentleness is in this withdrawal, which is accompanied by its secondary virtues: tact, subtlety, reserve, discretion. To not show ourselves, to set ourselves aside, and to guard ourselves are crowned by the last mystery that allows thinking, a certain suspension of identity.

The artificial is not even sad anymore; sorrows, regrets, expectations are erased by it. Advertisement reigns as trompe l'oeil. It amuses us with a certain refinement in the pursuit of pleasure. First we are dispossessed of our heartbreak, our distress. Memories are prohibited. Everything repeats itself in a loop, without heaviness or tears. Here lightheartedness is required, and we are relieved of a past filled with suspicious violence, unnecessary anxiety; and efforts to resuscitate it are in vain. We are invited to enter noiselessly into a space that offers in its permanent savagery the sensation of an artificial delicacy.

The artificial is unique in that it has no constraints. No adjuvant to the law, even if it were a codex. Each is freed from having to choose, there is no gap, no hesitation, no surprise. Voluntary servitude is the law, here calm reigns. The hallways of solitary confinement wards in psychiatric hospitals are just as quiet. We move with assurance into this world. No writing, no verdict, no judge, no prisoner—nothing transgresses anything. There is no place *other* than the artificial. The horizon line loops around itself. The very idea of a way out would be devastating; therefore, it does not exist. Justice is meaningless because there is nothing to transgress. All eroticism may disappear; the very idea of desire would be strange. Desiring comes with epiphany, loss, thirst, expectation, dizziness, skin, caress, fall, suspense. Gentleness. The artificial is self-regulated by its subjects without any need for exterior recourse to ensure this. They have been relieved of unnecessary grief, of anxious expectation, of sensibility. A name, like a gender, which each one of us bears, is a loan; you can keep it or get rid of it; you may be designated by a mere indefinite and neutral pronoun. The body is a resolved problem. The outcome after all is known; the boundless calls not for crime but for cruelty. In the artificial, gentleness doesn't mean anything, since there is nothing to hope for and nothing to dread because everything can resume and restart to infinity. The artificial has no reverse side, it leaves no way out.

EXHAUSTION

In order to hope for gentleness, we must ultimately have enough strength. Occasionally we lose hope. Wearing out gradually, silently. There are some blank lives that show no exterior signs of their own destruction except that they consist of absence—to self, to others, to the world. The desire that we feel for gentleness comes from an even more ancient time. From a relationship to the other that preceded our entrance into language.

We don't know what the lack of gentleness causes. Words trampled; bodies mistreated, left lifeless, sucked dry; sad passions—but above all charred emotions, pure existential ashes that cannot be brought back to this side of life. In order to ignore this void we fabricate satisfactions that we use as compensations. In some other cases, we will (unconsciously or not) exonerate him or her whom we expect to provide gentleness but don't (unconsciously or not) and excuse them regardless. We confront this lack with alibis, perjury, excuses, and pretexts. We blame it for our desertions. It is no longer unbearable; it simply discourages us from living. Today what we call "depression" is one of the major ways we deny our need for gentleness. With the best intention, we each create for the other a narrative about our own opacity. We have made exchange into a religion, yet we exchange nothing. What remains the most abrasive is sentimentalization, which in reality has come to hate emotion. Because emotion is always also thought. And encourages freedom. Our sensory receptors are brutalized; we collectively come to accept the unjustifiable. There is a brutality in the conditions of material survival; there is a spiritual and emotional desert where beings are trapped. The lack of gentleness is endemic. It has created a form of isolation as potent as a curse. No wealth, no sentimental reassurance can break it.

PENUMBRA

We have never concealed so much, but we do so under pretense of the constraint of total transparency that is the political form of "obscenity." But gentleness cannot occur under this rule of exhibitionism. Penumbra is its native land. There is a gentleness within trouble, within ambiguity, in what is born, in what emerges and claims this nascent and suspended space. The crude light of confession is not suitable for it. The general feeling of conspiracy or of the pervertibility of beings comes with a sense that any secret space privately bears some deviance and ought to be confessed immediately upon request. In a moment of paranoia, anything that isn't obscene in the way it unveils itself will be suspect, as will gentleness.

The lack of gentleness is viral. It spreads like poison. If we deprive the melancholic of his tears, that is, his purpose, he will be tempted to make himself disappear just when we think he is cured. He will retreat into the limbo from which his existence never wholly escaped, like the damned in Dante's hell. Renouncing nostalgia demands a courage that may sometimes fail. He certainly lacked gentleness too early on. Weaning is impossible when the gift was insufficient. Neglected children understand this. Those who had to become parents for their own parents so early endured the sacrifice in their stead, without anyone looking on during the crises. They kept quiet, squared their shoulders, succeeded brilliantly (since they were forgotten) or thoroughly failed (since they were forgotten). Their dereliction is not visible except to themselves. When the game of existence falls in on itself—and when protection has altogether disappeared, this lack of gentleness makes anxiety intolerable. The human machine might adjust, they may have a successful career, but those who depart from themselves to the point of denying that this very lack exists will feel the grip tighten slowly around their throats. Gentleness occurs at the moment when this sense of fatality gives way to an observation, however tenuous, of what we see, what we touch, what we hear, what we taste. It can defeat the intimate terror.

"MASTER AND MAN," BY TOLSTOY

It is a cold December night. A master and his servant set out on a path through the forest. Snow begins to fall; gradually it covers everything. They manage somehow to lead the sleigh forward, but the horse pulls it into a ditch and freezes. The cold overtakes them gradually. The master understands that all is lost. And something changes dramatically within him. Tolstoy,[33] without ever moralizing or dramatizing the scene, instead allows the whiteness of the snow to permeate and numb the whole tale until the moment when, let's call it gentleness, enters the master's heart. And we then see him holding his servant to his own body, warming him with his coat, and allowing himself to die in his place. Gentleness operates in the very seat of authority. It comes to rest in the interstices of cruelty and turns them inside out like a glove. It appears precisely where it is least expected. This type of gentleness is Christlike, insofar as one accepts Christ as the figure that reverses all attributes of authority into willing servitude; for example, Christ washing the feet of his disciples, an infinitely humane gesture, begins where neither explanation nor justification is possible. In the sleigh it is no longer a question of indulgence, patience, or justice. There are no witnesses other than the wolves in the distance, the cold, the snow, and the night. Nothing will be known of the spiritual struggle or the surrender.

THE SENSORY CELEBRATION (III)

Joy is one of the names of gentleness.

Chardin's white, milk, candle, clarity that suffuses darkness and spreads, sweeps away heaviness; lifts opacity. An antecedent clarity. This is perhaps one of the characteristics of gentleness, to be antecedent. Not a quality of being but of pure presence. The blue in Piero della Francesca's *Madonna del Parto.* The blue of this fresco is a mark that brings mystery into a bright night.

Gentleness belongs above all to the palate, to the newborn's memory of suckling. The sweet taste of sugar is its universal metaphor.[34] Sweetness and honey. It is the scent of milk, of figs, of roses; it is all the beloved scents that remind us of our early body, a body before the body— spiritual as well as sensorial and not yet confined by the tyranny of self-consciousness and the supervision of an era that craves thrills.

Gentleness opposes passion and the game of narcissistic mirrors that passion encourages. There is a power in gentleness that, far from temperance or tepidness, might carry in its wake a fervor that is another name for ecstasy.

Gentleness is a carnal as well as a spiritual quality, an erotic quality, whose intelligence of the other's desire seeks neither capture nor constraint, but the open play of the full range of perception.

Gentleness is a relationship to time that finds in the very pulsation of the present the feeling of a future and a past reconciled, that is, of a time that is not divided. This reconciled time makes life possible. The intimate revolution of gentleness holds the potential [*en puissance*] for a timeless freedom that transcends the boundaries of repetition and melancholia. Of animality, it keeps the taste and touch, the presence and grace. And in what it radiates, the essential presence of childhood.

There can be gentleness in fear.

Gentleness softens skin, vanishing into the very texture of things, of light, of touch, of water. It reigns in us through tiny fragments of time; giving space; removing the weight of shadows.

A swing. Head over heels, the world upside down. Pure bliss. The gentleness of back and forth.

It is a rhythm like the poem is an interior rhythm of language, a beat off-beat, a syncopated intonation. The nonfamiliar element within the familiarity of language. The verses of Baudelaire or Rimbaud have a peculiar gentleness because the savagery or the harshness of reality that they expose is delivered in a new, blossoming language that nothing can tame, not even after five hundred and thirty-four readings, and this spontaneous, vertiginous nature of the images shares with gentleness a mutual and secret measurelessness. Gentleness connects the spiritual and the material, the most subjective intention and the world's most objective intrusion, intelligence and ignorance, one and the other. It sews the world together like a poem that pulls back the folds of reality but without reconciling them.

SUBLIMATION

> Men who can most be moved by their passions are able
> to savor the most gentleness in this world.
> —RENÉ DESCARTES

Is gentleness a form of sublimation? Freud speaks of sublimation when the representation of the drive no longer
finds a satisfactory outlet and then consents to change
its object. The Freudian vocabulary is not that of the al-
chemist but that of the neurobiologist of his time, with
its expected rigidity and the ever-widening discrepancy
inflicted by the staggering discoveries made by the neu-
rosciences. We have changed scales; nanotechnologies
have come to the point of entering our bodies, assisting
each organ and reading the genome with increasing pre-
cision. But Freud was also a visionary, a sociologist, an
anthropologist, and a researcher. He ceaselessly chal-
lenged his own hypotheses. When he proposes the no-

tion of sublimation, he investigates what enables the drive to yield to the pleasure principle even in the case of failure; he strives to observe the trajectory followed by the actualization of desire, its "how," in a sense, rather than its "why." What is sublimated is primarily sexual energy, libido. The word "sublimation" itself already indicates an attraction to beauty or perfection. What's lost in this construction is the sexual itself; the only remaining sense of the body is the shadow cast by a desire restrained in its momentum. The discourse, the image, the arabesque of a dancer's step and the *lied* are ellipses whose secret and constantly avoided forge is sexuality. Sublimated desire requires that the very place from which it comes be abolished. From this perspective, gentleness culturally sublimates the violence and brutality of our most archaic animal reflexes: from vociferation to whisper.

As power, gentleness is not sublimation in the sense of a life drive that strives to always preserve the conditions of its own fulfillment. What it sublimates is the very access to the living. A gentleness drive?

CRUELTIES

It is a refined cruelty that Dostoevsky uncovers in the human soul. Piotr Stepanovich, Stavrogin's damned soul in *The Devils*, embodies shame, baseness, and treason but also cynical, elegant, and refined meanness. The profound pleasure of doing evil.[35] In this respect the seminal scene of Kirilov's murder/suicide is the seminal moment when pure reality is revealed in all its horror. The evil he sows around him comes from his inability to bond with others. As Heitor de Macedo remarks in a yet unpublished seminar dedicated to the novel, "To some extent Stravogin is beyond good and evil. Unaltered and unalterable, he ceaselessly attacks bonds as soon as they form. The bonds remain virtual and unacknowledged as such, weaving an exchange between him and the other."[36] An animal of unbelievable power, he seduces the men and women who cross his path, having raped and driven a little girl to suicide, but in his confession he admits that not a single thought was ever enough to save him from boredom; Stravogin is an inverted Christ figure. A rare example of humanity that redemption brushes up against without ever reaching. Even when face to face with the monk Ticcone or faced with the love that Chatov gives him, he can do nothing. The sublime character Lisa fails to reach him. She is not armed against evil. She tries to turn things around by offering herself to him, and when she is confronted with his lie, she goes and gets herself killed by the frenzied crowd. No salvation is possible, such is the reality. And yet there is a gentleness in Stravogin. A gentleness of extreme savagery. A gentleness to the extent that he moves forward while exposing himself all the time, such as he is, openly transgressing laws and customs, and without any of the false pretenses held by his contemporaries. By participating in a duel without ever aiming at his adversary, by biting the governor's ear by way of response, by pushing to suicide, to murder, to cowardice those donning the highest ideals of the Russian revolution, he lays bare all the abjection that he in fact embodies without self-awareness.

Stravogin is a Byronic figure whose motto would be, "Defeat yourself and you shall defeat the world." It is impossible for him to admit that thought cannot do everything. Nor can he let go of his pain, the only thing the subject possesses—for it gives him substance.

Absolute receptivity is the condition for the other's thinking. It is a necessary asceticism. An operation that will broaden life and the field of possibilities. Being a bearer of thought is a responsibility; the question of good and evil is posed at exactly that moment. In itself, gentleness, which shares numerous contiguities with joy, is no protection against evil; it can even be its vehicle. Evil does not necessarily coincide with the consciousness of evil. It is even heterogeneous to it; it raises itself to the ideal, to goodness, in order to patiently turn the effectiveness of goodness and the ideal against itself and therefore destroy any possibility for life. The temptation of self-destruction begins with life itself. Gentleness is also the temptation of the executioner. The infinitesimal progression from love to hatred: how does one become an executioner? It is not true that one day it takes hold of you and you pull the trigger, even when authorized and in times of war. You will have certainly consorted with evil before. Gentleness topples into horror because it has always sheltered horror. Did this pact start in infancy?

Cruelty is an attack carried out against what envelops the living growing into its own life and allowing for the conditions of its autonomy, its freedom, its elevation. Cruelty crushes the possible by asphyxiating to the bone the fragile protection that is an irrigation and a medium, literally a "transport." It reaches the heart by pretending to attack only the exterior, the skin. For otherness is the primary offense that feeds cruelty. There are murderous remarks uttered in a gentle voice; there are forms of violence feigning caress in order to reach the heart better.

IN HELL

The devastation that occurred in the twentieth century has a name: Shoah; every being is implicated by his or her history, filiation, thought. It is where the unnamable pushes beyond the limits we had previously assigned to evil. None of us has recovered from this trauma yet, even if we think we are far from it temporally, familially, historically. Such planning is the monstrous face of a murderous ideology of technology and betrayal. Every act of barbarism is based on a betrayal.

At the heart of our history, there is Nazism, the bomb, genocides, mass deportations. When survival hangs on a gesture, however tenuous it may be, what does gentleness become—so close to death? Each one of us bears this memory. We can no longer welcome the speech of a being whose family history is his sole horizon. In it we must collect the traces of the grand history, the shadows of devastation, the signs of collective traumas, and the periods of silence and forgetting.

"Penetrated by passive gentleness, he has, thus, something like a presentiment—remembrance of the disaster which would be the gentlest want of foresight. We are not contemporaries of the disaster: that is its difference, and this difference is its fraternal threat."[37] Disaster has no escape; it spreads like a bad omen and undermines history from within. It is a process on which no promise is grafted; it proclaims that trauma is something that remains to be thought, not only individually but also collectively. That it may be "the gentlest want of foresight" is only possible because we are not its contemporaries. When a trauma occurs, it defeats the very possibility of being a subject within it—except in rare exceptions, when lucid witnesses can confront it for what it is without being crushed. Something devastating falls upon us, preventing us from being brothers.

And yet that is when it is most crucial to summon gentleness. During World War I the genius war psychiatrist W. H. R. Rivers was assigned to the "regeneration" of soldiers who, seized by hallucinations and anxiety, collapsed on the battlefield. Neither deserters nor cowards, they could not be executed. They had to be cured . . . so they could be sent back to the front lines to fight. The task was grueling. The men were feeling, in their body and psyche, the blast that had cut their comrades in half; they kept replaying the scene in a fixed present and kept with them the constant anesthetizing smell of blood. They were among the living damned. For these beings Rivers proposed a listening that recreated the reliability of a human bond based on proximity, the ability to promise, and compassion. What he offered them was neither redemption nor a possible escape, but words that would come to give shelter to the memory of the dead and recreate space for life among the living.

LISTENING

"But there is, in my view, no grandeur except in gentleness" (Simone Weil). I will say rather: nothing extreme except through gentleness. Madness through excess of gentleness, gentle madness.

—MAURICE BLANCHOT

A psychoanalyst never listens without gentleness, even when he is abrupt. Gentleness participates in a gesture that invites the other. Perhaps at times he may hear nothing, perhaps he may daydream or be distracted or be furious with the person facing him, compelling him to stay there. Perhaps he will understand nothing about the story being told him, nothing about what the other's face or voice reveals.

The fact remains that what gives rise to listening is the possibility of an emotion complicit in connecting with what the other is not aware of in himself. The attention (sometimes free-floating) that the psychoanalyst gives to the one who is speaking, complaining, suffering, faltering, is a particular attention to details: tone of voice, images arising from a moment's hesitation, attitude, words oddly assembled, language tics. He attributes as much intelligence to them as to what they signify. His apparent immobility, his gently pressing silence, his thoughts; nothing betrays his distress. He resists the complaint invading the space and primarily the body of the other that is there in front of him, addressing its mortification to him. He resists the story distilled into the same refrain at their regular meetings, he even resists the urge to know. He tries to *hear* differently, to drive away the ghosts.

The complaint constantly expresses lack: of truthful words, of sex, of recognition, of honor. The complaint is no longer even a complaint; it is used until it is threadbare. Trauma, the history of wars, forgetting, distortions and gaps—what constitutes a new origin is interwoven in a matrix of silences that will claim their rights. The resistance of the analyst is a struggle, in each and every session, every inch of the way, against the inner torturer that treats him as an adversary. The patient doesn't know this is the case but sometimes guesses it. It is the patient who is subjected to the yoke of this deceptively gentle tyranny of the superego that constantly interferes between others and himself, making each event a repetition of a past. This Sadean master decides what is true and what isn't, doable or not, and the analyst is powerless as he witnesses this dismemberment. A true massacre. In the name of what we should be—or worse: should have been; again a massacre of this past conditional that makes of the past a living reproach. How does one manage to complain, session after session, and find an excuse every single time? Trying to convince oneself that this really is about fate; the psychoanalyst becomes the participating witness of a script already written. And the torturer mocks this witness and smiles at his benevolence.

The psychoanalyst hears this lack of gentleness. On what shore must we stand in order to believe that we can change what is called "fatality"? The perception of gentleness comes afterward. A boundary breached, a death overcome, a forbidden border stepped over, shamelessly. That is when it can occur. It acts, comes to disrupt the encounter. Diverting speech when unpredictable truths emerge. Then a balm of gentleness pours in. It is a state of grace that doesn't last. But regardless, it will have taken place. It is for these moments that the analyst is there. He has already made a passage in his listening for what has appeared between words, between signs, in the interstices of a dream, of a silence, of a fear audible in breathing too quickly. The micro-dissonances, the breaks in cadence. In this river of a voice that carries suffering and affliction, there are unknown, forgotten passages, these are the passages that dreams follow in order to reach us, these are the passages that are ravished by vision and haunted by insomnia.

We are committed beyond ourselves. Perception infinitely more vast than everything we assume about the psyche that monitors and regulates our behavior. Gentleness does not have time, it is time itself. It encompasses temporality as a whole; hence the feeling of reminiscence that reaches us in its presence. It's unfortunate that we need so much time in order to realize that we will have looked for an escape that does not exist, that has no place; a pure reflection, a mirage. That the only thing that counts is the how, the encounter with the self—that is to say, with what spans and establishes a life, an idea of justice, a way to love, to give.

Gentleness visits us. We never manipulate it or possess it. We must accept entering its tides, treading its hollow paths, getting lost so that something unprecedented may arise. You could say that gentleness lodges itself in this tenuous, fracturable space where what occurs does so with your consent, even though you can't understand or grasp it within the boundaries of your former self.

How can we listen to so much pain without giving in to sadness ourselves? There is within sadness a form of passion that is difficult to part with once it has taken hold. How do we welcome wonder? The unspeakable is the space of a struggle that we have deserted, sometimes a very long time ago. Time does not pass in this domain called "the unconscious." Within ourselves the simultaneity of events occurs without respite or reparation—grief is at the source of an experience that can't be represented or spoken but can only return, spectrally. Haunting us in this tenuous and insistent form of sadness. The analyst knows that there is something inconsolable about what this man cannot say in this moment, this man who nevertheless has come here seeking solace. Or at least, from the analyst's listening, gentleness. It may be the other name for what welcomes part of this unconsoled grief, frozen in a time that no story will ever recount. He will simply need to be there and share the wait. The man speaks of a separation that is impossible to overcome, of a woman that he left without giving it too much thought and who now haunts him. He doesn't understand this grief, this weight of memory. He does what needs to be done and even more, but nothing is able to conquer the sadness. He speaks of this "bygone era" when something he did not see was decided without his knowing.

The power of listening is a suspended realization. Awaiting completion. Words miss what they designate. What is said is constantly measured against the unformulable that secretly supports these words. In his listening, the psychoanalyst tries to reach what cannot be said, tries to hear the hesitations, the emotion holding back other words that are forbidden, erased.

Aristotle writes that there is in nature a perfection to the realization of power. Every living thing can be understood in this way. We must accept its force. Understanding that what escapes—the untranslatable, what can never be brought to language—is so precisely what has allowed for there to be words, language, rhythm, rituals. It is the core (so it is called) of the rope around which the rest is woven.

It is not one and the other who are listening to each other; it is actually listening that is unfolding between them. This gentleness arises because it connects two strangers who have become intimate; once or twice a week, same time, same place. These strangers were once children whose thoughts, imagination, fears, longing, amazement, feelings of love are lodged in fragments of light in the body, in words, in what lights up their eyes. The power of listening is an activator, in the folds—as understood by Deleuze—of the psyche that are micro-recorders of the real.

Listening watches over the unexpected.

Isn't listening the gentlest expression of the unexpected, of chance, of encounter? What reaches you beyond the limits prescribed by your imagination. The undreamed of takes root in hope and undoes it at the same time it accomplishes it. It is a quality of the real. Perhaps the most gentle quality; is this why we want to avoid breaking in at all costs?

Gentleness is an essential detour with space itself in countershot. There is no road, no sign, no map of the landscape. Mental space comes at this cost: bringing back what you know, betting on the unnamable. Relying on the remainder of night that surrounds us, before civilization, before language, before rituals.

TRAUMA AND CREATION

Gentleness is what turns traumatic intrusion into creation. It is what, during the haunted night, offers light; during mourning, a beloved face; during the collapse of exile, the promise of a shore on which to stand. So this is how light enters, making a stronger imprint than the desire to return, stronger than the lost object of melancholy or renunciation.

In order to approach and indeed to heal from trauma, we need to be able to go as far as where our body was hurt. We must sew another skin over the burn left by the event. Create a protective covering *ad minima* without which liberation is impossible lest the trauma haunt the individual's life. Gentleness is one of the conditions of this reconstruction.

Trauma is negative rapture. The subject is raptured from himself; his ego is no longer in control; it is swept away, uprooted; something takes hold of it and leads it back to this moment of existence when it was neither constituted nor constructed, yet already entirely existed. Trauma is subversion that demands exile. Ignoring this paves the way for all depressions—from the most radical plan of renunciation to latent postpartum depression. And medication only patches up the desire to live, or the heartache, or the professional failure, or the feeling of inadequacy; for nothing can sew up such a wound. Nothing except creation, what reopens the wound elsewhere and differently, but on less shifting ground.

Gentleness can come when traumatic pain ceases. This return to the freedom of a nonviolated body and to healthy words is already a creation. It rediscovers primitive sensations from the origin of desire, and perhaps also the origin of time. Leaving trauma behind frees us from the constraints exerted by pain. Convalescence offers a flavor that is in itself a kind of miracle that can only be savored this one time.

BEYOND THE CONFINES

There is the gentleness of a mother toward her child, a lover's caress, that of an animal; there is the gentleness of an atmosphere and that of a state of mind. The subtlety comes from the precious within each of these occasions. What is touched, or kept, or felt diffuses a quality that is difficult to define in the moment, but that suffuses the real with light. The right distance as invented by gentleness allows everyone to exist within his or her own space; it is the opposite of intrusion.

What do we call this savage part of ourselves that goes beyond the confines of this withdrawal that we call "being alone," the beginning of this life that is chosen and not merely endured?

CLANDESTINE GENTLENESS

> Beneath any carnal attraction which is at all profound,
> there is the permanent possibility of danger.
>
> —MARCEL PROUST

Sneaking in [*en douce*]. Under the table. Invisible, gentleness lets itself be forgotten. As discreet and essential as a heartbeat.

Leaving unnoticed [*en douce*]. A narrow escape. Gentleness maintains a few exclusive affinities with secrecy. It aids the lovers' night, their flight from public radars.

Operating *on the* sly [*en douce*], taking orders from no one.

No event in this world is foreign to gentleness because gentleness bears the responsibility of language. Without gentleness, there is no being in the world of language. Children translate overwhelming emotion into words. They repeat, they babble, they echolize; "mama" is the first word of almost every child on this planet, a word that for the infant denotes gentleness. Taming the world is made possible through language as soft as a comforting whisper. Between waking and dreaming, the world is sung about and placed surreptitiously [*en douce*] within those first words.

A clandestine figure of what glides by covertly. Gentleness is an anarchist idea that has entered furtively [*en douce*] into a law book, undermining its entire structure.

Surveillance has become routine. Everything can track our actions, our movements, our phone conversations, our desires, our friends. It makes gentleness "turn sour" like milk.

Gentleness lurks. Lying in wait. Near the end of his life Freud hypothesized that the death drive was foundational. Below the line of human bondage: hate.[38] Collectively and individually, we are survivors of a long traumatic history. I don't think hate is enough to survive on.

Gentleness comes into the garden by night. Darkness, like blindness, reveals touch. Where the hand becomes entirely thinking, gentleness begins there too, secretly.

There is not a secret that was always there, only waiting to be revealed (that only happens in children's books); there is no Pandora's box to be opened; only the pure movement of life.

Suddenly a small fox appears. It comes to drink the turquoise water in the morning light. The animal heads for the opposite bank and disappears. From the eucalyptus trees comes a fragrance of crumpled leaves and tangerine. In the stealth of the wild animal, there is the glimmer of a gentleness never before captured.

Eroticism is the invention of a music that was never practiced. In eroticism what belongs to ritual, to litany is paradoxically clandestine. There is gentleness in this repeated taming of savagery, of biting, sometimes of brutality, even when it is desired. In itself the ritual expresses a form of secret recognition, tacit and free.

THE SENSORY CELEBRATION (IV)

Stubble grass, steep ground, barren rosebushes in the winter light. A robin makes its nest in the rosebush; it appears every day at approximately the same time. We shouldn't pay too much attention to things, only contemplate them in their essential imbalance from time to time; then, gently, they reveal a secret.

Nature holds all things in memory, and yet it is an absolute present, translucent, letting through everything it does not reflect: light, night, cold, snow. Winter beach cold sand, short sharp waves; four laughing girls playing volleyball, their hair flying; their whole lives nestled here, gathered within their bodies, intact. Without knowing it. Sand slipping through their fingers; tiny pieces of glass polished and worn by the sea, lukewarm to the touch of the hand picking them up. Sand still cold from the night before and from an ancient time, seemingly unaware of death, buried deep under the stones, light, the disappearing voices of children.

Snow becomes gentleness with the evening sun.

An apricot-colored cardigan, the sign of sensuality itself; a child's fetishism.

White sky, not a single shadow left anywhere. Open arms whirling in the snow. No more up or down. Thin, fragmented slivers of light.

A perfume, an instant. A bathroom cupboard left ajar by a curious child. A bottle knocked over. Cinnamon, amber, and something else; no one is unaffected by such a memory. You think of all the possible lives suddenly made present by a smell. Round, tender. It restores the contours to things, since they only exist through this colorless density. All at once, a perfume evoking a skin, an atmosphere, freeing in the memory what moves through us but doesn't belong to us.

Gentleness has an astonishing connection to thought.

A feeling of weightlessness that it shares with cosmonauts, comets. Gentleness liberates skin from being skin, it doesn't resonate, it merges, it winds itself around the lines of the landscape; it doesn't dampen anything, it gives space to things and removes the weight of shadows.

Gentleness hides inside the voices of exile; it finds there an echo of its passage and the ungraspable lightness in the tessitura of a voice.

To experience the world gently, as if our senses were raw.

Anxiety comes into the body when gentleness abandons it.

We should speak of skies desperately bright, dry, where gentleness is lacking. Of moods comparable to skies, when we are internally exiled, when nothing seems to touch us.

Gentleness is calm. It radiates from the eye of the storm, witnessing its unchained forces and remaining untouched itself. Calm is a supreme power.

You play with the little girl who moves the nativity figurines on the floor like knights on an invisible chessboard. The sheep, the goat, the manger, the wise man. So many constellations in our private sky. This time shared with the child is infinitely precious. It creates thought and world within the self, it places this shadow of our expectation somewhere, in a sheltered place. Gentleness, it is the movement of the child's hand, seizing the blue and white stucco dove, laying it by the ribbon (the ribbon becomes a river with a ceramic bridge above it and an immobile shepherdess crossing it), and moving the dove slightly, just to see. This time is not there for anything except the pure event of being together.

The gentleness of illness and convalescence, of time stretching out infinitely, of a time made boundless with the unreal sensation brought on by fever. The contours of the real fade away; what remains in us, like a very light sediment of the world itself, is the pure sensation of existence.

CHILDHOOD

Gentleness has in common with childhood an ability to permeate the past without leaving more of an imprint than most lived events.

Gentleness belongs to childhood; it is its secret name. The pleasure that the child discovers, exploring and tasting, is an experience of the world that will be the reservoir of his secret attachments. The world will not change languages for the adult that the child will become. The exquisite gentleness of one afternoon by the water is encapsulated forever in every experience with similar light. We would not survive childhood without gentleness because everything about childhood is so exposed, hyperacute, in a way violent and raw, that gentleness is its absolute prerequisite.

We do not recover from our childhood without choosing life, consciously, a second time. Being born is not enough. The joys, the expectations, the troubles of childhood are events that compose us with an intensity that will set the tone for our entire existence. In that sense childhood is entirely "traumatic," not because it is tragic but because it reaches psychological realms within us primarily through perception and sensibility. And to be entirely there without remainder is rare and is becoming more rare as our scattered, fragmented self takes over, as absence to ourselves becomes the rule.

Gentleness comes with the possibility of life; with uterine envelopment that filters emotions, sounds, and thoughts; with amniotic fluid; with the touch on the other side of one's skin; with closed eyes that cannot yet see; with breathing still protected from the aggression of the air. Without the gentleness of this original touch we would not be in the world. The touch of gentleness undoubtedly sleeps in each one of our cells, beckoning us to return, impossibly, to this lost world that rocked us long before maternal arms did. The world of childhood prolongs gentleness; this is why the image of a little child sleeping is one of the universal images of gentleness, as if the aura of innocence and the very infinity of body and skin, the confidence and the total surrender demonstrated by this body, recall the primal surrender from whence we came.

GENTLENESS OF MELANCHOLY

But isn't there also, in melancholy, the attraction of a deadly gentleness?

Anguish is born like a tune whose melody gradually infiltrates and overwhelms every other sound. The disturbing regularity that characterizes it (the same hours of the day or night), once it has us in its grip, conjures up a space of absolute savagery that we cannot approach rationally. Anxiety will not be tamed. It pervades space and makes any recognition impossible; we no longer see how the horizon could open, we only see its closed line. Anguish is a death threat precisely when we should accept it as part of being mortal and therefore as part of being ephemeral—not belonging, being transhumant on this earth. It brings a slight misalignment in space and time that suddenly leaves us in the most complete disarray. The body knots itself. Then the idea comes that everything could be in vain, that there would no longer be a part to play, no longer any openings on the chessboard.

When we are seized by the feeling that nobody will ever come to us, that this solitude will not loosen its grip on us, ever, we must still find the strength to extend our arms, to kiss, to love. To say it, to start again, to hear the whisper of that wild voice that calls you from well before your beginnings.

Ordinary melancholy wreaks havoc. In its wake it does not announce the deadly color it dons; it takes on simpering airs; it pretends to be sadness, then emptiness, then exhaustion, and finally when the lure of death appears, nobody saw or understood anything. We are left alone like this. Medication, doctors, distraught family, it is the same old story: "You have to pull yourself together." The melancholy person clings to his lost object until the end, resuming this forever repaired, ravaging death. He wants to devour it, shred it, use it for his own pleasure. One would then in a sense have to stir up the disease to find health again.

Gentleness sometimes informs the decision to consent to the worst: to mourning, for example. This ageless sadness, what inside of us also belongs to the missing, the absent, is coiled up, interwoven inside the body and in the hollow of the throat. Is it possible to pass through melancholy? "Thus the shadow of the object fell upon the ego," writes Freud.[39] Might gentleness be deadly? Yes, in melancholy as in sleep, snow, water: all the way to complete self-oblivion. Disconnection, the illusion of total disconnection.

DOLCE VITA

> For good people, consenting feels sweet because they
> recognize the good in itself, and what good people feel
> in respect to themselves, they also feel with respect to
> their friends. . . . One must therefore "consent" that
> this friend exists, and this happens by living together
> and by sharing acts and thoughts in common.
>
> —GIORGIO AGAMBEN

It is not always sweet [*doux*] to live. But the sensation of
being alive calls upon gentleness.

The image of Anita Ekberg entering the Trevi
Fountain fully clothed while being watched by the
gaze of an astonished man and by us remains etched
in memory as that of a life that invites us to gentleness, but also to madness, to dancing freedom, and to
sensuality.[40]

In the sweet life [*douceur de vivre*] there is a temperate atmosphere, neither too hot nor very cold, the same temperature as the body. There have been such climates throughout History.

The sweet life [*douceur de vivre*] left its mark on the Renaissance and found its apogee in the eighteenth century with the art of conversation, the sharing of ideas, the secret of carnal celebration, the desire for liberty. It was a way of thinking about the world, being friendly with the erotic and theorized body; this was an art of the garden, of architecture, of light. Wonder was not only a fantasy, but also a way of experiencing reality.

In every era, the sweet life was embodied in the lifestyles of certain people or certain communities, but often in secret. The sweet life [*douceur de vivre*] is not regarded with adequate benevolence, because it is irresistibly drawn to what takes risks outside norms, obligations, and imposed judgments; it is a reverence for what in the very principle of life doesn't obligate itself.

When new forms of language, new ways of loving renew our relationship with the world, for example, in film, in painting, in mores, and in the literature of the interwar period, the sweetness of life becomes this new relationship's private and secret ferment.

Is the sweet life a state of grace or the fruit of continuous diffusion? Might it also be the visible moment of a long, slow metamorphosis of which freedom is the secret pendulum? At what distance must we place ourselves to make such an evaluation? Is the sweet life achievable at all, or is our only option to resist being crystallized by living in one of the forms of resentment (Nietzsche again), of dejection, of identity crisis, and of all the ensuing forms of fear? How can our era acclimate to what the power of gentleness offers us, the possibility not only of the kindness toward self that it implies but also of the spiritual and carnal momentum that animates it?

A GENTLE REVOLUTION

O nomen dulce libertatis—Sweet name of liberty

—CICERO

It is sometimes inadvertently that a revolution takes place. An effect of extreme gentleness, barely different from other moments, and then life suddenly catches fire, is ablaze. But burning with inexplicable gentleness. As if suddenly you were taken by the hand along a precipice and needed not only to walk along the edge but to dance, and yes, you dance without fear or vertigo as if the very space took refuge in you, and then as if, upon arriving on the other side, everything had changed, but without violence. Is the intimate revolution of this kind? This is what makes it so difficult to think about, to transcribe, to capture. It is a spiral that leads you to an unexpected height when verticality lays bare an unknown path, an elevation that creates a need for air, in a space traveled a hundred times ad nauseam, in the repetition of days, attitudes, words.

Gentleness is a return to self that invents a future in the image of the spiral. An open revolution. It is a "repetition" in the sense intended by Kierkegaard: reviving the past with a view to a possible opening to the unexpected. If one believes in working with the unconscious, returning to self is not merely remembering. Because memory concerns a past self that no longer exists in the form of a still indeterminate present self. The repetition will be, like the Nietzschean *amor fati*, a consented return to the past that, by this acquiescence, would find the extent of its secret power. To understand or hear oneself is not without effect. Gentleness is one of the names of this reconciliation with what has been repressed, exiled in the past and therefore "repeated" with indulgence and the courage that it takes to admit that we were there, in conscience.

Gentleness is what allows us to reach out to this stranger who comes to us, in us. It is the voice that the poet collects and animates. It is placed there as part of the wild world. Because we harbor it within ourselves, it takes great gentleness to tame even a few moments of the stranger's intrusion. Madness (today called psychosis) is the prolonged ambush of this otherness becoming sovereign. Sometimes in order to escape from lies that have persisted for generations.

A young Italian was drafted into the army during the First World War. For months he hid in the mountains with his comrades. They had almost no provisions left. The order was to defend the mountain pass at any cost. Feeling a sense of absurdity that he tried to hide from the others, he kept a journal. One night he noticed the movement of troops in the pass on the other side of the cliffs separating the narrow valley, and he thought that all was lost. The offensive would occur the very next day, that much was certain, and he knew he and his comrades would not have enough ammunition. That night, without his comrades knowing, he decided to venture as close as possible to the enemy camp. Halfway there he almost turned back; he heard a song rising from a gramophone. The surprise held him. He was so moved by it that he decided to come forward until he was seen in the open, a sign of surrender in his hand. He was captured immediately and brought to the officer of the German army. The record was still playing. They both knew the tune. The voice that rose from the recording had an unusual gentleness. The German officer talked with this man all night. Risking everything, the Italian explained the position of his troops, their certain death, and put their fate completely in his hands. The German officer let him leave in the morning. And he never launched the attack. He went in the direction of another valley, leaving them time to withdraw and make their escape. This is a story of gentleness.

NOTES

1. Fyodor Dostoyevsky, *The Idiot*, trans. Richard Pevear and Larissa Volokhonsky (New York: Vintage, 2003).

2. Knut Hamsun, *Hunger*, trans. Robert Bly (New York: Farrar, Straus & Giroux, 1967).

3. J. Meade Falkner, *Moonfleet* (Boston: Little, Brown, 1951).

4. Jan Patočka, *Essais hérétiques*, trans. Erika Abrams (Paris: Verdier, 1981), 92–93; translation ours.

5. "*Potency* means: (1) the principle of motion or of change that is a thing other than the thing moved or changed, or in the thing moved or changed but qua other"; Aristotle, *Metaphysics*, trans. Hippocrates G. Apostle (Bloomington: Indiana University Press, 1966), Book V, chap. 12, 87.

6. "Each thing, as far as it lies in itself, strives to persevere in its being"; Baruch Spinoza, *Ethics* (New York: Hafner, 1949), part 3, prop. 6.

7. Friedrich Nietzsche, *The Gay Science* (Cambridge and New York: Cambridge University Press, 2001), Book V, §349.

8. [English in the original.—Trans.]

9. 1 Corinthians 4.21.

10. Matthew 5.5.

11. Jacqueline de Romilly, *La Douceur dans la Pensée Grecque* (Paris: Les Belles Lettres, 1979).

12. Aeschylus, "The Eumenides," in *The Oresteia*, trans. Robert Fagles (New York: Penguin, 1984).

13. Sophocles, *Ajax,* trans. R. C. Trevelyan (London: G. Allen & Unwin, 1919), part 1, cell 1.

14. Plato, *Symposium*, 189c–d, Aristophanes's Speech, 520, §193d.

15. [Platon, *Apologie de Socrate.*—Au. Translation ours.—Trans.]

16. Plato, *Laws*, Book VI, trans. Benjamin Jowett, in *The Dialogues of Plato* (Oxford: Oxford University Press, 1892), 138, §757e.

17. Ibid., 113, §731.

18. [In English in the original text.—Trans.]

19. Aristotle, *Nicomachean Ethics*, trans. David Ross (Oxford and New York: Oxford University Press, 2009), IV, 6, §1126a, 74.

20. In the sense of the French "par-donner"; see Jacques Derrida, *On Cosmopolitanism and Forgiveness*,

trans. Mark Dooley (London and New York: Routledge, 2001).

21. Plutarch, *Life of Solon*, in *Plutarch's Lives*, trans. Aubrey Stewart and George Long (Philadelphia: George Bell, 1880), vol. 1, part VII.

22. Augustine, *Confessions*, trans. J. G. Pilkington (New York: Horace Liveright, 1927), Book IX, chap. 1, 188.

23. Saint Francis of Assisi, *Testament*, in *The Writings of Saint Francis of Assisi*, trans. Paschal Robinson (Philadelphia: Dolphin, 1906), 81–86, 152–53.

24. Sri Vallabha-acharya, *The Sweetness of Lord Sri Krishna*, translator unknown, 1478 A.D., text 1, accessed August 9, 2017, http://www.harekrsna.de/madhurastakam-e.htm.

25. [François Jullien, *Les Transformations silencieuses* (Paris: Grasset, 2009).—Au.]

26. Ibid., 187.

27. Marguerite Duras, *The Atlantic Man*, in *Two by Duras*, trans. Alberto Manguel (Toronto: Coach House, 1993), 58.

28. Tolstoy, *The Kingdom of God Is Within You*, trans. Constance Garnett (Lincoln and London: University of Nebraska Press, 1984), chap. 9.

29. Henry David Thoreau, *Civil Disobedience*, in *Walden and Civil Disobedience* (New York: Norton, 1966), part 1, §4.

30. Victor Hugo, *The Man Who Laughs*, trans. unknown (Boston: Little and Brown, 1888), 363, 278, 150.

31. Flaubert's letter to Mme Roger Genette, June 19, 1876; Flaubert, *Correspondance* (Paris: Charpentier et Fasquelle, 1893), IV:233–34; translation ours.

32. Emmanuel Levinas, *Totality and Infinity: An Essay on Exteriority*, trans. Alphonso Lingis (Pittsburgh: Duquesne University Press, 1969), 257–58.

33. Leo Tolstoy, *"Master and Man" and Other Parables and Tales*, ed. Ernest Rhys (London: Dent; New York: Dutton, 1910). The author's footnote refers to the French translation: *Maître et serviteur.*

34. [*Douceur* also means *dessert* or *sweet treat.*—Trans.]

35. [Pleasure=*Jouissance.*—Trans.]

36. Heitor de Macedo, *Séminaire La Clinique de Dostoïevski: Les démons, 2012–2013*; translation ours.

37. Maurice Blanchot, *The Writing of the Disaster*, trans. Ann Smock (Lincoln: University of Nebraska Press, 1986), 5.

38. ["Below the line of human bondage: hate"; in English in the original text.—Trans.]

39. Freud, *Mourning and Melancholia*, in *The Complete Psychological Works of Sigmund Freud*, trans. James Strachey (London: Hogarth Press, 1914), vol. XIV, 249.

40. Federico Fellini, *La Dolce Vita*, Pathé, 1960.

INDEX